THE
EGYPTIAN
BOOK
OF THE
DEAD

Translated by E. A. Wallis Budge

CLASSICS

Published 2025

FiNGERPRINT! CLASSiCS
Prakash Books

f Fingerprint Publishing
X @FingerprintP
@ @fingerprintpublishingbooks
www.fingerprintpublishing.com

ISBN: 978 93 6214 931 2

A JOURNEY THROUGH
THE UNDERWORLD

"But the sun rises again when the night is past, and, as it begins a new life with renewed strenght and vigour, it became the type of the new life which the Egyptian hoped to live in the world beyond the grave."

Mystery, magic, and the promise of eternity these are the hallmarks of The Egyptian Book of the Dead. Known in ancient Egypt as The Book of Coming Forth by Day, this text is not a "book" in the modern sense but a collection of spells, prayers, and incantations designed to guide the deceased through the perilous journey of the afterlife. It is a profound testament to the ancient Egyptians' belief in the interconnectedness of life, death, and rebirth.

Imagine a world where death is not the end but a portal to an even greater existence. For the ancient Egyptians, the afterlife was a mirror of the earthly realm, yet free from suffering. However, reaching this paradise required navigation through trials, tests, and encounters with divine entities. It was a journey fraught with challenges: lakes of fire, gates guarded by serpents, and the final judgment before Osiris, the god of the underworld. To the Egyptians, being equipped with the knowledge and words of power within this book was as essential as breath in life.

Composed over centuries, this text was inscribed on papyrus scrolls, tomb walls, and even the wrappings of mummies. Each version was unique, tailored to the individual's needs and station in life. Some included only a few spells, while others were richly adorned with detailed illustrations—vibrant depictions of the afterlife, from lush fields to formidable demons. These artworks not only offered visual guidance but also underscored the Egyptians' artistic brilliance and spiritual depth.

What makes this ancient text truly fascinating is its seamless blend of spirituality and practicality. It serves not only as a guide through the afterlife but also as a reflection of the ancient Egyptians' profound understanding of existence. Their belief system emphasized harmony and balance—ideals personified by the goddess Ma'at, whose feather of truth determined a soul's worthiness for eternal life.

Even thousands of years later, The Egyptian Book of the Dead continues to captivate scholars, artists, and seekers of wisdom. Its influence can be seen in modern depictions of the afterlife and our ongoing fascination with ancient Egypt. Whether you approach it as a historical artifact, a spiritual guide, or a literary masterpiece, this book will be an unparalleled journey into the ancient heart of life, death, and the eternal beyond.

PREFACE

The Papyrus of Ani, which was acquired by the Trustees of the British Museum in the year 1888, is the largest, the most perfect, the best preserved, and the best illuminated of all the papyri which date from the second half of the XVIIIth dynasty (about B.C. 1500 to 1400). Its rare vignettes, and hymns, and chapters, and its descriptive and introductory rubrics render it of unique importance for the study of the Book of the Dead, and it takes a high place among the authoritative texts of the Theban version of that remarkable work. Although it contains less than one-half of the chapters which are commonly assigned to that version, we may conclude that Ani's exalted official position as Chancellor of the ecclesiastical revenues and endowments of Abydos and Thebes would have ensured a selection of such chapters as would suffice for his spiritual welfare in the future life. We may therefore regard the Papyrus of Ani as typical of the funeral book in vogue among the Theban nobles of his time.

The first edition of the Facsimile of the Papyrus was issued in 1890, and was accompanied by a valuable

Introduction by Mr. Le Page Renouf, then Keeper of the Department of Egyptian and Assyrian Antiquities. But, in order to satisfy a widely expressed demand for a translation of the text, the present volume has been prepared to be issued with the second edition of the Facsimile. It contains the hieroglyphic text of the Papyrus with interlinear transliteration and word for word translation, a full description of the vignettes, and a running translation; and in the Introduction an attempt has been made to illustrate from native Egyptian sources the religious views of the wonderful people who more than five thousand years ago proclaimed the resurrection of a spiritual body and the immortality of the soul.

The passages which supply omissions, and vignettes which contain important variations either in subject matter or arrangement, as well as supplementary texts which appear in the appendixes, have been, as far as possible, drawn from other contemporary papyri in the British Museum.

The second edition of the Facsimile has been executed by Mr. F. C. Price.

E. A. WALLIS BUDGE
BRITISH MUSEUM
January 25, 1895

CONTENTS

1.	PLATE 1	9
2.	PLATE 2	21
3.	PLATE 3	23
4.	PLATE 4	26
5.	PLATES 5–6	32
6.	PLATE 7	47
7.	PLATES 11–12	61
8.	PLATE 13	78
9.	PLATE 14	81
10.	PLATE 15	84
11.	PLATE 16	91
12.	PLATE 17	101
13.	PLATE 18	105
14.	PLATE 19	109
15.	PLATE 20	113

16.	PLATE 21	116
17.	PLATE 22	119
18.	PLATES 23–24	122
19.	PLATE 25	124
20.	PLATE 26	128
21.	PLATE 27	132
22.	PLATE 28	137
23.	PLATES 29-30	140
24.	PLATES 31-32	147
25.	PLATE 32 (continued)	156
26.	PLATES 33–34	168
27.	PLATES 35–36	174
28.	PLATE 37	176

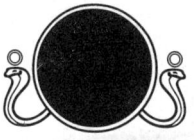

PLATE

1

Vignette: The scribe Ani, standing with hands raised in adoration before a table of offerings consisting of haunches of beef, loaves of bread and cake, vases of wine and oil, fruits, lotus, and other flowers. He wears a fringed white and saffron-coloured linen garment; and has a wig, necklace, and bracelets. Behind him stands his wife "Osiris, the lady of the house, the lady of the choir of Amen, Thuthu," similarly robed and holding a sistrum and a vine branch in her right hand, and a *menat* in her left.

A HYMN OF PRAISE TO RA WHEN HE RISETH IN THE EASTERN PART OF HEAVEN. Behold Osiris Ani the scribe who recordeth the holy offerings of all the gods, who saith: "Homage to thee, O thou who hast come as Khepera, Khepera, the creator of the gods. Thou risest, thou shinest, making bright thy mother [Nut], crowned king of the gods. [Thy] mother Nut doeth homage unto thee with both her hands. The land of Manu receiveth thee with content, and the goddess Maat embraceth thee at the two seasons. May he give splendour, and power, and triumph, and a coming-forth [*i.e.*, resurrection] as a living soul to see Horus of the two horizons to the *ka* of Osiris, the scribe Ani, triumphant before Osiris, who saith: Hail all ye gods of the Temple of the Soul, who weigh heaven and earth in the balance, and who provide food and abundance of meat. Hail Tatunen, One, creator of mankind and of the substance of the gods of the south and of the north, of the west and of the east. Ascribe [ye] praise unto Ra, the lord of heaven, the Prince, Life, Health, and Strength, the Creator of the gods, and adore ye him in his beautiful Presence as he riseth in the *atet* boat. They who dwell in the heights and they who dwell in the depths worship thee. Thoth and Maat both are thy recorders. Thine enemy is given to the fire, the evil one hath fallen; his arms are bound, and his legs hath Ra taken from him. The children of impotent revolt shall never rise up again.

The House of the Prince keepeth festival, and the sound of those who rejoice is in the mighty dwelling. The gods are glad [when] they see Ra in his rising; his beams flood the world with light. The majesty of the god, who is to be feared, setteth forth and cometh unto the land of Manu; he maketh bright the earth at his birth each day; he cometh unto the place where he was yesterday. O mayest thou be at peace with me; may I behold thy beauties; may I advance upon the earth; may I smite the Ass; may I crush the evil one; may I destroy Apep in his hour; may I see the *abtu* fish at the time of his creation, and the *ant* fish in his creation, and the *ant* boat in its lake. May I see Horus in charge of the rudder, with Thoth and Maat beside him; may I grasp the bows of the *seket* boat, and the stern of the *atet* boat. May he grant unto the *ka* of Osiris Ani to behold the disk of the Sun and to see the Moon-god without ceasing, every day; and may my soul come forth and walk hither and thither and whithersoever it pleaseth. May my name

PLATE 1

be proclaimed when it is found upon the board of the table of offerings; may offerings be made unto me in my presence, even as they are made unto the followers of Horus; may there be prepared for me a seat in the boat of the Sun on the day of the going forth of the god; and may I be received into the presence of Osiris in the land of triumph!

Appendix: The following versions of this chapter are taken from: I. Naville, *Todtenbuch*, Bd. I., Pl. xiv.

A HYMN OF PRAISE TO RA WHEN HE RISETH IN THE EASTERN PART OF HEAVEN. Behold Osiris, Qenna the merchant, who saith: "Homage to thee, in thy rising thou Tmu in thy crowns of beauty. Thou risest, thou risest, thou Ra shinest, thou shinest, at dawn of day. Thou art crowned like unto the king of the gods, and the goddess Shuti doeth homage unto thee. The company of the gods praise thee from the double-dwelling. Thou goest forth over the upper air and thy heart is filled with gladness. The *sektet* boat draweth onward as [Ra] cometh to the haven in the *atet* boat with fair winds. Ra rejoiceth, Ra rejoiceth. Thy father is Nu, thy mother is Nut, and thou art crowned as Ra-Harmachis. Thy sacred boat advanceth in peace. Thy foe hath been cast down and his head hath been cut off; the heart of the Lady of life rejoiceth in that the enemy of her lord hath been overthrown. The mariners of Ra have content of heart and Annu rejoiceth."

The merchant Qenna saith: "I have come to thee, O Lord of the gods, Tmu-Harmachis, who passest over the earth I know that by which thou dost live. Grant that I may be like unto one of those who are thy favoured ones [among the followers] of the great god. May my name be proclaimed, may it be found, may it be lastingly renewed with The oars are lifted into the *sektet* boat, and the sacred boat cometh in peace. May I see Ra when he appeareth in the sky at dawn, and when his enemies have fallen at the block. May I behold

11

[Horns] guiding the rudder and steering with [his] two hands. May I see the *abtu* fish at the moment of his creation; and may I see the *ant* fish when he maketh himself manifest at creation, and the *ant* boat upon its lake. O thou Only One, O thou Mighty One, thou Growing One, who dost never wax faint, and from whom power cannot be taken. the devoted servant of "the lord of Abtu."

"The merchant Qenna saith: "Homage to thee Heru-Khuti-Tmu, Heru-Khepera, mighty hawk, who dost cause the body [of man] to make merry, beautiful of face by reason of thy two great plumes. Thou wakest up in beauty at the dawn, when the company of the gods and mortals sing songs of joy unto thee; hymns of praise are offered unto thee at eventide. The starry deities also adore thee. O thou firstborn, who dost lie without movement, arise; thy mother showeth loving kindness unto thee every day. Ra liveth and the fiend Nak is dead; thou dost endure for ever, and the fiend hath fallen.

"Thou sailest over the sky with life and strength. The goddess Nehebka is in the *atet* boat; the sacred boat rejoiceth. Thy heart is glad and thy brow is wreathed with the twin serpents."

A HYMN OF PRAISE TO RA WHEN HE RISETH IN THE EASTERN PART OF HEAVEN. Behold Osiris, Qenna the merchant, triumphant, who saith: "Homage to thee, O thou who risest in Nu, and who at thy birth dost make the world bright with light; all the company of the gods sing hymns of praise unto thee. The beings who minister unto Osiris cherish him as King of the North and of the South, the beautiful and beloved man-child. When he riseth, mortals live. The nations rejoice in him, and the Spirits of Annu sing unto him songs of joy. The Spirits of the towns of Pe and Nekhen exalt him, the apes of dawn adore him, and all beasts and cattle praise him with one accord. The goddess Seba overthroweth thine enemies, therefore rejoice within thy boat; and thy mariners

12

PLATE 1

are content thereat. Thou hast arrived in the *atet* boat, and thy heart swelleth with joy. O Lord of the gods, when thou dost create them, they ascribe praises unto thee. The azure goddess Nut doth compass thee on every side, and the god Nu floodeth thee with his rays of light. O cast thou thy light upon me and let me see thy beauties, me, the Osiris Qenna the merchant, triumphant! When thou goest forth over the earth I will sing praises unto thy fair face. Thou risest in the horizon of heaven, and [thy] disk is adored [when] it resteth upon the mountain to give life unto the world."

Saith Qenna the merchant, triumphant: "Thou risest, thou risest, coming forth from the god Nu. Thou dost become young again and art the same as thou wert yesterday, O mighty youth who hast created thyself. Not my hand. Thou hast come with thy splendours, and thou hast made heaven and earth bright with thy rays of pure emerald light. The land of Punt is established for the perfumes which thou smellest with thy nostrils. Thou risest, O thou marvellous Being, in heaven, the twin serpents are placed upon thy brow, and thou art lord of the world and the inhabitants thereof; [the company] of the gods and Qenna the merchant, triumphant, adore thee."

A HYMN OF PRAISE TO RA WHEN HE RISETH IN THE EASTERN PART OF HEAVEN. Behold Osiris Hunefer, triumphant, who saith: "Homage to thee, O thou who art Ra when thou risest and Tmu when thou settest. Thou risest, thou risest; thou shinest, thou shinest, thou who art crowned king of the {p. 251} gods. Thou art the lord of heaven, [thou art] the lord of earth, [thou art] the creator of those who dwell in the heights and of those who dwell in the depths. [Thou art] the One god who came into being in the beginning of time. Thou didst create the earth, thou didst fashion man, thou didst make the watery abyss of the sky, thou didst form Hapi [the Nile], and thou art the maker of streams and of the great deep, and thou givest life to all that is therein. Thou hast knit together the mountains, thou has made mankind and the beasts of the field, thou hast created the heavens and the earth. Worshipped be thou whom the goddess Maat embraceth at morn and at eve. Thou dost travel across the sky with heart swelling with joy; the Lake of Testes is at peace. The fiend Nak hath fallen and his two arms are cut off. The *sektet* boat receiveth fair winds, and the heart of him that is in his shrine rejoiceth. Thou art crowned with a heavenly form, the Only one, provided [with all things]. Ra cometh forth from Nu in triumph. O thou mighty youth, thou everlasting son, self-begotten, who didst give thyself birth, O thou mighty One, of myriad forms and aspects, king of the world, Prince of Annu, lord of eternity and ruler of the everlasting, the company of the gods rejoice when thou risest and when thou sailest across the sky, O thou who art exalted in the sektet boat. Homage to thee, O Amen-Ra, thou who dost rest upon Maat, thou who passest over the heaven, and every face seeth thee.

Thou dost wax great as thy Majesty doth advance, and thy rays are upon all faces. Thou art unknown and canst not be searched out ... his fellow except thyself; thou art the Only One ... [Men] praise thee in thy name [Ra], and they swear by thee, for thou art lord over them. Thou hast heard with thine ears and thou hast seen with thine eyes. Millions of years have gone over the world; I cannot tell the number of them, through which thou hast passed. Thy heart hath decreed a day of happiness in thy name [of Ra]. Thou dost pass over and travellest through untold spaces of millions and hundreds of thousands of years; thou settest out in peace, and thou steerest thy way across the watery abyss to the place which thou lovest; this thou doest in one little moment of time, and thou dost sink down and makest an end of the hours."

Osiris, the governor of the palace of the lord of the two lands (*i.e.*, Seti I.), Hunefer, triumphant, saith: Hail my lord, thou that

PLATE 1

passest through eternity and whose being is everlasting. Hail thou Disk, lord of beams of light, thou risest and thou makest all mankind to live. Grant thou that I may behold thee at dawn each day."

A HYMN OF PRAISE TO RA by Nekht, the royal scribe, captain of soldiers, who saith: "Homage to thee, O thou glorious Being, thou who art provided [with all things]. O Tmu-Heru-khuti, when thou risest in the horizon of heaven, a cry of joy cometh out of the mouth of all peoples. O thou beautiful Being, thou dost renew thyself in thy season in the form of the Disk within thy mother Hathor; therefore in every place every heart swelleth with joy at thy rising, for ever. The eastern and the western parts of heaven come to thee with homage, and give forth sounds of joy at thy rising. O Ra, thou who art Heru-khuti (Harmachis), the mighty man-child, the heir of eternity, self-begotten and self-born, king of earth, prince of the netherworld, governor of the mountains of Aukert (i.e., the netherworld), thou dost rise in the horizon of heaven and sheddest upon the world beams of emerald light; thou art born from the water, thou art sprung from Nu, who fostereth thee and ordereth thy members. O thou who art crowned king of the gods, god of life, lord of love, all the nations live when thou dost shine. The goddess Nut doeth homage unto thee, and the goddess Maat embraceth thee at all times. They who are in thy following sing unto thee with joy and bow down to the earth when they meet thee, the god of heaven, the lord of earth, the king of right and truth, the god of eternity, the everlasting ruler, the prince of all the gods, the god of life, the creator of eternity, the maker of heaven by whom is established all that therein is. The company of the gods rejoice at thy rising, the earth is glad when it beholdeth thy rays; the peoples that have been long dead come forth with cries of joy to see thy beauties. Thou goest forth over heaven and earth, made strong each day by thy mother Nut. Thou passest through the uppermost heaven, thy heart swelleth with joy; and the Lake of Testes is content thereat. The Enemy hath fallen, his arms are hewn off, the knife hath cut asunder his joints. Ra liveth in Maa the beautiful. The *sektet* boat draweth on and cometh into port; the south, the north, the west and the east turn to praise thee, O thou unformed substance of the earth, who didst create thyself. Isis and Nephthys salute thee, they sing unto thee in thy boat hymns of joy, they shield thee with their hands. The souls of the East follow thee, the souls of the West praise thee. Thou art the ruler of all gods and thou hast joy of heart within thy shrine; for the Serpent Nak is condemned to the fire, and thy heart shall be joyful for ever. Thy mother Nut is adjudged to thy father Nu."

PLATE

2

Vignette I.: The disk of the Sun, supported by a pair of arms proceeding from the ankh, the sign of life, which in turn is supported by a *tet* the emblem of the East and of the god Osiris. The *tet* stands upon the horizon. On each side of the disk are three dog-headed apes, spirits of the Dawn, their arms raised in adoration of the disk. On the right hand side of the *tet* is the goddess Nephthys and on the left is Isis each goddess raising her hands in adoration of the *tet*, and kneeling upon the emblem *aat*, or hemisphere.

Above is the sky. This vignette belongs properly to the hymn to the rising sun.

HYMN TO OSIRIS: "Glory be to Osiris Un-nefer, the great god within Abydos, king of eternity, lord of the everlasting, who passeth through millions of years in his existence. Eldest son of the womb of Nut, engendered by Seb the Erpat, lord of the crowns of the North and South, lord of the lofty white crown. As Prince of gods and of men he hath received the crook and the flail and the dignity of his divine fathers. Let thy heart which is in the mountain of Amenta be content, for thy son Horus is stablished upon thy throne. Thou art crowned lord of Tattu and ruler in Abtu. Through thee the world waxeth green in triumph before the might of Neb-er-tcher. He leadeth in his train that which is and that which is not yet, in his name Ta-her-seta-nef; he toweth along the earth in triumph in his name Seker. He is exceeding mighty and most terrible in his name Osiris. He endureth for ever and for ever in his name Un-nefer. Homage to thee, King of kings, Lord of lords, Prince of princes, who from the womb of Nut hast possessed the world and hast ruled all lands and Akert. Thy body is of gold, thy head is of azure, and emerald light encircleth thee. O An of millions of years, all-pervading with thy body and beautiful in countenance in Ta-sert. Grant thou to the *ka* of Osiris, the scribe Ani, splendour in heaven and might upon earth and triumph in Neter-khert; and that I may sail down to Tattu like a living soul and up to Abtu like a *bennu* (phœnix); and that I may go in and come out without repulse at the pylons of the Tuat. May there be given unto me loaves of bread in the house of coolness, and offerings of food in Annu, and a homestead for ever in Sekhet-Aru with wheat and barley therefor."

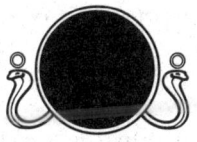

PLATE

3

Vignette: Scene of the weighing of the Heart of the Dead. Ani and his wife enter the Hall of Double Law or Truth, wherein the heart, emblematical of the conscience, is to be weighed in the balance against the feather, emblematical of law. Above, twelve gods, each holding a sceptre are seated upon thrones before a table of offerings of fruit, flowers, etc. Their names are: Harmachis, "the great god within his boat"; Tmu; Shu; Tefnut, "lady of heaven"; Seb; Nut, "lady of Heaven" Isis; Nephthys; Horus, "the great god"; Hathor, "lady of Amenta"; and Sa. Upon the beam of the scales sits the dog-headed ape which was associated with Thoth, the scribe of the gods. The god Anubis, jackal-headed, tests the tongue of the balance, the suspending bracket of which is in the form of the feather The inscription above the head of Anubis reads:—"He who is in the tomb saith, pray thee, O weigher of righteousness, to guide (?) the balance that it may be stablished." On the left of the balance, facing Anubis, stands Ani's "Luck" or "Destiny," *Shai* and above is the object called *mesxen* which has been described as "a cubit with human head," and which is supposed to be connected with the place of birth. Behind these stand the goddesses Meskhenet and Renenet: Meskhenet presiding over the birth-chamber, and Renenet probably superintending the rearing of children. Behind the *meskhen* is the soul of Ani in the form of a human-headed bird standing on a pylon. On the right of the balance, behind Anubis, stands Thoth, the scribe of the gods, with his reed-pen and palette containing black and red ink, with which to record the result of the trial. Behind Thoth stands the female monster Amam, the "Devourer," or Am-mit, the eater of the Dead."

Osiris, the scribe Ani, saith: "My heart my mother, my heart my mother, my heart my coming into being! May there be nothing to resist me at [my] judgment; may there be no opposition to me from the *Tchatcha*; may there be no parting of thee from me in the presence of him who keepeth the scales! Thou art my *ka* within my body [which] knitteth and strengtheneth my limbs. Mayest thou come forth to the place of happiness to which I am advancing. "May the *Shenit* not cause my name to stink, and may no lies be spoken against me in the presence of the god! Good is it for thee to hear." . . .

Thoth, the righteous judge of the great company of the gods who are in the presence of the god Osiris, saith: "Hear ye this judgment. The heart of Osiris hath in very truth been weighed, and his soul hath stood as a witness for him; it hath been found true by trial in the Great Balance. There hath not been found any wickedness in him; he hath not wasted the offerings in the temples; he hath not done harm by his deeds; and he uttered no evil reports while he was upon earth."

The great company of the gods reply to Thoth dwelling in Khemennu: "That which cometh forth from thy mouth hath

PLATE 3

been ordained. Osiris, the scribe Ani, triumphant, is holy and righteous. He hath not sinned, neither hath he done evil against us. Let it not be given to the devourer Amemet to prevail over him. Meat-offerings and entrance into the presence of the god Osiris shall be granted unto him, together with a homestead for ever in Sekhet-hetepu, as unto the followers of Horus."

PLATE

4

Vignette: Ani, found just, is led into the presence of Osiris. On the left the hawk-headed god Horus, the son of Isis, wearing the double crown of the North and the South, takes Ani by the hand and leads him forward towards "Osiris, the lord of eternity" *Ausar neb t'etta*, who is enthroned on the right within a shrine in the form of a funereal chest. The god wears the *atef* crown with plumes; a *menat* hangs from the back of his neck; and he holds in his hands the crook, sceptre, and flail, emblems of sovereignty and dominion. He is wrapped in bandages ornamented with scale work. The side of his throne is painted to resemble the doors of the tomb. Behind him stand Nephthys on his right hand and Isis on his left. Facing him, and standing on a lotus flower, are the four "children of Horus (*or* Osiris)," or gods of the cardinal points. The first, Mestha, has the head of a man; the second, Hapi, the head of an ape; the third, Tuamautef, the head of a jackal; and the fourth, Qebhsennuf, the head of a hawk.

PLATE 4

Suspended near the lotus is an object which is usually called a panther's skin, but is more probably a bullock's hide.

The roof of the shrine is supported on pillars with lotus capitals, and is surmounted by a figure of Horus-Sept or Horus-Seker and rows of uraei.

In the centre Ani kneels before the god upon a reed mat, raising his right hand in adoration, and holding in his left hand the *kherp* sceptre. He wears a whitened wig surmounted by a "cone," the signification of which is unknown. Round his neck is a deep collar of precious stones. Near him stands a table of offerings of meat, fruit, flowers, etc., and in the compartments above are a number of vessels for wine, beer, oil, wax, etc., together with bread, cakes, ducks, a wreath, and single flowers.

Appendix: The shrine is in some instances represented in the shape of a pylon, the cornice of which is ornamented either with uraei, or with the disk of the sun and feathers, emblematic of Maat. It usually rests upon a base made in the shape of a cubit, The throne upon which Osiris sits is placed upon reed mats or upon the cubit-shaped base, or in a pool of water, from which springs a lotus flower with buds and having the four gods of the cardinal points standing upon it. In some of the oldest papyri the body of Osiris is painted white, and he stands upright. Isis is described as "great lady, divine mother," and Nephthys as "the mistress of the underworld." In the Papyrus the scene of the presentation of the deceased to Osiris is unusual and of interest. On the right the scribe Nekht and his wife Thuau stand with both hands raised in adoration of Osiris. Behind them, upon a cubit-shaped base, is a house with four windows in its upper half, and upon the roof two triangular projections similar to those which admit air into modern houses in the East. Before the door are a sycamore tree and a palm tree, with clusters of fruit; on the left is the god Osiris on his throne, and behind him stands "Maat, mistress of the two countries, daughter of Ra," above whom are two outstretched female arms proceeding from a mountain and holding a disk between the hands. In the centre, between Osiris and the deceased, is a pool of water with three sycamore trees on each side, and at each corner a palm tree bearing clusters of dates; and from it there springs a vine laden with bunches of grapes.

In the Papyrus the god seated in the shrine wears the crown of the god Tanen, and is called "Ptah-Seker-Ausar, within the hidden place, great god, lord of Ta-sert, king of eternity, prince of the everlasting."

Saith Horus, the son of Isis: "I have come unto thee, O Unnefer, and I have brought the Osiris Ani unto thee. His heart is [found] righteous coming forth from the balance, and it hath not sinned against god or goddess. Thoth hath weighed it according to the decree uttered unto him by the company of the gods; and it is very true and righteous. Grant him cakes and ale; and let him enter

PLATE 4

into the presence of Osiris; and may he be like unto the followers of Horus for ever."

Behold, Osiris Ani saith: "O Lord of Amentet (the underworld), I am in thy presence. There is no sin in me, I have not lied wittingly, nor have I done aught with a false heart. Grant that I may be like unto those favoured ones who are round about thee, and that I may be an Osiris, greatly favoured of the beautiful god and beloved of the lord of the world, the royal scribe indeed, who loveth him Ani, triumphant before the god Osiris."

Appendix: The usual title of this chapter is,

"Chapter of not allowing the heart of [the deceased] to be driven away from him in the underworld." it is an address by the deceased to his own heart, which he calls his *ka* or "double" within his body. It should be accompanied by a vignette of the trial of the heart in which the heart is weighed against the dead man himself, as in the ancient Nebseni papyrus.

In the Ani papyrus, however, it will be observed that the heart is being weighed against the feather of the Law, Maat, a scene which often accompanies Chapter

Interesting variants of the vignettes of Chapter XXXB. are given by Naville (*Todtenbuch*, Bd. I., Bl. 43), where we find the deceased addressing either his heart placed on a stand, or a beetle, or a heart to which are attached the antennae of a beetle. In certain papyri this chapter is followed by a rubric:—"[This chapter is] to be said over a scarab of green stone encircled with *smu* metal, and [having] a ring of silver, which is to be placed upon the neck of the dead. This chapter was found in Khemennu.

Written upon a slab of steel of the South, in the writing of the god himself, under the feet of the majesty of the god, in the time of the majesty of Men-kau-Ra, the king of the North and of the South, triumphant, by the royal son Heru-tata-f who found it while he was journeying to inspect the temples."

The scarabs which are found in the mummies, or lying upon the breast just above the position of the heart, form an interesting section of every large Egyptian collection. In the British Museum series every important type of the funereal scarab is represented. They are made of green basalt, green granite white limestone light green marble black stone, blue paste, blue glass and purple, blue, or green glazed *faïence*. They vary in size from 5 inches to 2 inches in length. On the hard stone examples the text of the Chapter of the Heart, more or less complete, is usually cut on the base in outline; but it is sometimes traced in red ink or in gold. Incuse hieroglyphics are sometimes filled with gold. The name of the person with whom the scarab was buried usually precedes the text of the Chapter of the Heart; but in many instances blank spaces are found left without insertion of the name—a proof that i, these amulets were bought ready-made. The base however is often quite plan or figures of Osiris, Isis, and Nephthys occupy the place of the usual inscription. The backs of scarabs are generally quite plain, but we find examples inscribed with figures of the boat of the Sun Osiris, with flail and crook the *bennu* bird, and the *u'tat* Ra and

PLATE 4

Osiris, and the *bennu* bird with the inscription *neteri ab en Ra*, "the mighty heart of Ra" A finehard, green stone scarab of the Greek or Roman period has upon the back the figures of four Greek deities. In rare instances, the beetles have a human face or head. Carefully made scarabs have usually a band of gold across and down the back where the wings join: an example of the late period has the whole of the back gilded. The scarab was set in a gold oval ring, at one end of which was a smaller ring for suspension from the neck or for attachment to the bandages of the mummy. The green glazed *faïence* scarab of Thothmes III was suspended by a gold chain from a bronze torque. The base of the scarab is sometimes in the form of a heart. At a period subsequent to the dynasty inscribed funereal scarabs in marble, paste, etc., were set in pylon-shaped pectorals made of Egyptian porcelain, glazed blue, green, or yellow, which were sewed to the mummy bandages over the heart. On such pectorals the boat of the Sun is either traced in colours or worked in relief, and the scarab is placed so as to appear to be carried in the boat; on the left stands Isis, and on the right Nephthys.

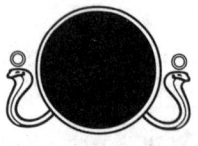

PLATES

5–6

Vignettes: The funereal procession to the tomb; running the length of the two plates. In the centre of Plate 5 the mummy of the dead man is seen lying in a chest or shrine mounted on a boat with runners, which is drawn by oxen. In the boat, at the head and foot of the mummy, are two small models of Nephthys and Isis. By the side kneels Ani's wife Thuthu, lamenting. In front of the boat is the *Sem* priest burning incense in a censer, and pouring out a libation from a vase; he wears his characteristic dress, a panther's skin. Eight mourners follow. one of whom has his hair whitened. In the rear a sepulchral ark or chest surmounted. by a figure of Anubis and ornamented with emblems of "protection" and "stability," is drawn on a sledge by four attendants, and is followed by two others. By their side walk other attendants carrying Ani's palette, boxes, chair, couch, staff, etc.

In Plate 6 the procession is continued up to the tomb. In the centre is a group of wailing women, followed by attendants carrying on yokes boxes of flowers, vases of unguents, etc. In the right centre are a cow with her calf, chairs of painted wood with flowers upon them, and an attendant with shaven head, carrying a haunch, newly cut, for the funereal feast. The group on the right is performing the last rites. Before the door of the tomb stands the mummy of Ani to receive the final honours; behind him, embracing him, stands Anubis, the god of the tomb; and at his feet, in front, kneels Thuthu to take a last farewell of her husband's body. Before a table of offerings stand two priests: the *Sem* priest, who wears a panther's skin, holding in his right hand a libation vase, and in his left a censer; and a priest holding in his right hand an instrument with which he is about to touch the mouth and eyes of the mummy, and in his left the instrument for "opening the mouth." Behind or beside them on the ground, in a row, lie the instruments employed in the ceremony of "opening the mouth," etc., the *mesxet* instrument, the sepulchral box, the boxes of purification, the bandlet, the libation vases, the ostrich feather and the instruments called *Seb-ur*, *Temanu* or *Tun-tet*, and the *Pesh-en-kef.* The *Kher-heb* priest stands behind reading the service of the dead from a papyrus.

Appendix: In the papyrus of Hunefer a slab or stele with rounded top is placed by the door of the tomb (Fig. 1, In the upper part of it the deceased is shown adoring Osiris, and below is the legend, "Hail, Osiris, the chief of Amenta, the lord of eternity, spreading out in everlastingness, lord of adorations, chief of the company of his gods; and hail, Anubis [dweller] in the tomb, great god, chief of the holy dwelling. May they grant that I may go into and come out from the underworld, that I may follow Osiris in all his festivals at the beginning of the year, that I may receive cakes, and that I may go forth into the presence of [Osiris]; I, the double (*ka*) of Osiris, the greatly favoured of his god, Hu-nefer. "In the upper register of this section of the papyrus is the text of the "Chapter of opening the mouth of the statue of Osiris." The complete scene, including this stele and vignette, appears in the tomb of Pe-ta-Amen-Apt. In the vignette of the first chapter of the Book of the Dead in the papyrus of Neb-qet the soul of the deceased is represented descending the steps of the tomb to carry food to its mummy in the underground chamber (Fig. 2).

FIG. 1.

FIG. 2.

The ceremonies which took place at the door of the tomb in an Egyptian funeral are of considerable interest. The priest called *Kher-heb*, holding the *Sem* priest by the arm, gives directions for the slaughter of "a bull of the South." The slaughterer, standing on the bull, cuts off a fore-leg (Fig. 3) and takes out the heart. A woman, called the *Tcherauur*, who personifies Isis, then whispers in the deceased's ear, "Behold, thy lips are set in order for thee, so that thy mouth may be opened." Next, an antelope and a duck are brought by order of the *Kher-heb*, and their heads are cut off. The *Kher-heb* then addresses the *Sem* priest: "I have seized them for thee, I have brought unto thee thine enemies. His hands bring his head [as] his gift. I have slain them for thee, O Tmu; let not his enemies rise up against this god." The slaughterer then presents the thigh to the *Kher-heb*, and the heart to an official whose title was *Smer*, and all three then "place the thigh and the heart upon the ground before this god" (*i.e.*, Osiris). The *Kher-heb* then says to the deceased, represented by his mummy or statue: I have brought unto thee the thigh (Fig. 4) as the Eye of Horus. I have brought unto thee the heart; let there be no rising up against this god. I have

FIG. 3.

brought unto thee the antelope, his head is cut off; I have brought unto thee the duck, his head is cut off." Here the sacrifice ends.

FIG. 4.	FIG. 5.	FIG. 6.

The next part of the ceremony, *i.e.*, "the opening of the mouth and eyes," is performed by the *Sem* priest, who addresses the deceased: "I have come to embrace thee, I am thy son Horus, I have pressed thy mouth; I am thy son, I love thee. His mother beats her breast and weeps for him, and those who are in chains with him (*i.e.*, Isis and Nephthys) beat their breasts. Thy mouth was closed, but I have set in order for "thee thy mouth and thy teeth." The *Kher-heb* next calls on the *Sem* priest four times: "O *Sem*, take the *Seb-ur* (Fig. 5) and open the mouth and the eyes"; and while the *Sem* priest is performing the ceremony the *Kher-heb* continues: "Thy mouth was closed, but I have set in order for thee thy mouth and thy teeth. I open for thee thy mouth, I open for thee thy two eyes. I have opened for thee thy mouth with the instrument of Anubis. I have opened thy mouth with the instrument of Anubis, with the iron tool with which the mouths of the gods were opened. Horus, open the mouth, Horus, open the mouth. Horus hath opened the mouth of the dead, as he whilom opened the mouth of Osiris, with the iron which came forth from Set, with the iron tool with which he opened the mouths of the gods. He hath opened thy mouth with it. The dead shall walk and shall speak, and his body shall [be] with the great company of the gods in the Great House of the Aged one in Annu, and he shall receive there the *ureret* crown from Horus, the lord of mankind." The *Kher-heb* next says: "Let the *Ami-Khent* priest (Fig. 7) stand behind him (*i.e.*, the deceased), and say, 'My father, my father,' four times." The eldest son of the deceased then stands behind the deceased, and in his name the *Kher-heb* says: "His mother beateth her breast and weepeth for him, and those who are in chains with him also beat their breasts."

FIG. 7.

FIG. 8.

Another priest, called *Am-Khent-Heru*, takes up the same position and says: "Isis goeth unto Horus, who embraceth his father." A priestly official belonging to the *mesenti* class then goes behind the deceased, and the *Sem*, *Smer* and *Kher-heb* priests stand in front, and the *Sem* priest and the *Kher-heb*, personifying Horus and Sut, respectively cry: "I am Horus, I am Sut; I will not let thee illumine the head of my father." The *Sem* priest then leaves the *Ka*-chapel and returns, leading in the *Se-mer-f*, *i.e.*, "the son who loveth him"; whereupon the *Kher-heb* says: "O Sem, let the *Se-mer-f* come into the tomb in order that he may see the god." The *Sem* priest holding him by the arm then leads forward the *Se-mer-f*, who addresses the deceased: "I have come, I have brought

37

unto thee thy son who loveth thee; he shall open for thee thy mouth and thine eyes." (Fig. 8). A tomb-official, *Am-as*, then takes up his position behind the deceased, and the *Se-mer-f* and the *Kher-heb* stand in front; the *Kher-heb* repeating four times: "The *Se-mer-f* openeth the mouth and the two eyes of the deceased, first with a needle of iron, then with a rod of *smu* metal"; the *Am-as* addressing the deceased: "Behold the *Se-mer-f*"; and the *Kher-heb* saying, in the name of the *Se-mer-f*: "I have pressed for thee thy mouth, even as thy father pressed it in the name of Seker. Hail, Horus hath pressed thy mouth for thee, he hath opened thine eyes for thee; Horus hath opened thy mouth for thee, he hath opened for thee thine eyes; they are firmly stablished. Thy mouth was closed; I have ordered thy mouth and thy teeth for thee in their true order. Thou hast [again] opened thy mouth; Horus hath opened thy mouth. I have stablished thy mouth firmly. Horus hath opened for thee thy mouth, Horus hath opened for thee thy two eyes." The *Kher-heb* then speaks on behalf of the *Sem* priest: "Thy mouth was closed up. I have ordered aright for thee thy mouth and thy teeth. Thy mouth is firmly stablished. Thy mouth was tightly closed. His mouth is firmly stablished, and [his] two eyes are firmly stablished." The *Sem* priest next presents to the deceased (Fig. 9) a cone-shaped offering, and at the same time the *Kher-heb* says: "Open the mouth and the two eyes, open the mouth and the two eyes. Thou hadst tightly closed thy mouth, thou hast [again] opened thy two eyes." Then the *Kher-heb* says, on behalf of the *Smer* (Fig. 10) priest who stands behind the deceased:

FIG. 9.	FIG. 10.	FIG. 11.

"One cometh unto thee for thy purification." Next the *Se-mer-f* comes forward with four boxes (Fig. 11) in his hands, and the *Kher-heb* says: "O *se-mer-f*, take the four boxes of purification, press the mouth and the two eyes, and open the mouth and the two eyes with each of them four times, and say, 'Thy mouth and thy two eyes are firmly stablished, and they are restored aright,' and say also, 'I have firmly pressed thy mouth, I have opened thy mouth, I have opened thy two eyes by means of the four boxes of purification.'" The *Sem* priest then approaches the deceased (Fig. 12) with the instrument ###, and the *Kher-heb* at the same time says: "O *Sem* priest, lay the *pesh-en-kef* upon his mouth, and say, 'I have stablished for thee thy two jaw-bones in thy face which was divided into two parts.'" The *Sem* priest next makes an offering of grapes (Fig. 13), the *Kher-heb* saying: "O *Sem* priest, place the grapes upon his mouth and say, 'He bringeth to thee the eye of Horus, he graspeth it; do thou also grasp it.'" After an ostrich feather has been offered (Fig. 14) by the *Sem* priest, and a number of the ceremonies described above have been repeated, and other animals slaughtered, the *Kher-heb* addresses the *Sem* priest, and says: "Take the instrument *Tun-tet* (thrice) and open the mouth and the eyes" (four times). He then continues: "O *Sem* priest, take the iron instrument of Anubis, *Tun-tet* (thrice). Open the mouth and the two eyes (four times), and say, 'I open for thee thy mouth with the iron instrument of Anubis with which he opened the mouths of the gods. Horus openeth the mouth, Horus openeth the mouth,

FIG. 12.

FIG. 13.

FIG. 14.

Horus openeth the mouth with the iron which cometh forth from Set, wherewith he hath opened the mouth of Osiris. With the iron tool (*meskhet*) wherewith he opened the mouths of the gods doth he open the mouth. He [the deceased] shall go in and he shall speak [again], and his body shall dwell with the company of the great gods in Annu, wherein he hath received the *ureret* crown from Horus, lord of men. Hail, Horus openeth thy mouth and thy two eyes with the instrument *Seb-ur* or *Teman*, with the instrument *Tun-tet* of the Opener of the Roads (*i.e.*, Anubis) wherewith he opened the mouth of all the gods of the North. Horus the Great cometh to embrace thee. I, thy son who loveth thee, have opened thy mouth and thy two eyes. His mother beateth her breast in grief while she embraceth him, and the two sisters (*i.e.*, Isis and Nephthys), who are one, strike themselves in grief. All the gods open thy mouth according to the book of the service.'" The *Kher-heb* next instructs the *Sem* priest to clothe the mummy or statue of the deceased with the *nemes* band or fillet (Fig. 15), and to say: "Lo! the *nemes* fillet, the *nemes* fillet, which cometh as the light, which cometh as the light; it cometh as the eye of Horus, the brilliant; it cometh forth from Nekheb. The gods were bound therewith; bound round is thy face with it in its name of *Hetch* (*i.e.*, light, or brilliance), coming forth from Nekheb. "All that could do harm to thee upon earth is destroyed." The *Sem* priest, holding a vase of ointment in his left hand, and smearing the mouth with his fore-finger (Fig. 16), says: "I have anointed thy face with ointment, I have anointed thine eyes. I have painted thine eye with *uatch* and with *mestchem*. May no ill-luck happen through the dethronement of his two eyes in his body, even as no evil fortune came to Horus through the overthrow of his eye in his body. Thy two eyes are decked therewith in its name of *Uatch*, which maketh thee to give forth fragrance, in its name of "Sweet-smelling." A number of scented unguents and perfumes are brought forward, and at the presentation of each a short sentence is recited by the *Kher-heb* having reference to the final triumph of the deceased in the underworld and to the help which the great gods will render to him.

FIG. 15.

HERE BEGIN THE CHAPTERS OF COMING FORTH BY DAY, AND OF THE SONGS OF PRAISE AND GLORIFYING, AND OF COMING FORTH FROM AND GOING INTO THE GLORIOUS NETER-KHERT IN THE BEAUTIFUL AMENTA; TO BE SAID ON THE DAY OF THE BURIAL: GOING IN AFTER COMING FORTH. Osiris Ani, Osiris, the scribe Ani, saith: "Homage to thee, O bull of Amenta, Thoth the king of eternity is with me. I am the great god in the boat of the Sun; I have fought for thee. I am one of the gods, those holy princes who make Osiris to be victorious over his enemies on the day of weighing of words. I am thy mediator, O Osiris. I am [one] of the gods born of Nut, those who slay the foes of Osiris and hold for him in bondage the fiend Sebau. I am thy mediator, O Horus. I have fought for thee, I have put to flight the enemy for thy name's sake. I am Thoth, who have made Osiris victorious over his enemies on the day of weighing of words in the great House of the mighty Ancient One in Annu. I am Tetteti, the son of Tetteti; I was conceived in Tattu, I was born in Tattu. I am with those who weep and with the women who bewail Osiris in the double land of Rechtet; and I make Osiris to be victorious over his enemies. Ra commanded Thoth to make Osiris victorious over his enemies; and that which was bidden for me Thoth did. I am with Horus on the day of the clothing of Teshtesh and of the opening of the storehouses of water for the purification of the god whose heart moveth not, and of the unbolting of the door of concealed things in Re-stau. I am with Horus who guardeth the left shoulder of Osiris in Sekhem, and I go into and come out from the divine flames on the day of the destruction of the fiends in Sekhem. I am with Horus on the day of the festivals of Osiris, making the offerings on the sixth day of the festival, [and on] the Tenat festival in Annu. I am a priest in Tattu, I Rere in "the temple of Osiris, [on the day of] casting Up the earth. I see the things which are concealed in Re-stau. I read from the book of the festival of the Soul [which is] in Tattu. I am the *Sem* priest, and I perform his course. I am the great chief of the work on the day of the placing of the *hennu* boat of Seker upon its sledge. I have grasped the spade on the day of digging the ground in Suten-henen. O ye who make perfected souls to enter into the Hall of Osiris, may ye cause the perfected soul of Osiris, the scribe Ani, victorious [in the Hall of Double Truth], to enter with you into the house of Osiris. May he hear as ye hear; may he see as ye see; may he stand as ye stand; may he sit as ye sit!

"O ye who give bread and ale to perfected souls in the Hall of Osiris, give ye bread and ale at the two seasons to the soul of Osiris Ani, who is victorious before all the gods of Abtu, and who is victorious with you.

"O ye who open the way and lay open the paths to perfected souls in the Hall of Osiris, open ye the way and lay open the paths to the soul of Osiris, the scribe and steward of all the divine offerings, Ani [who is triumphant] with you. May he enter in with a bold heart and may he come forth in peace from the house of Osiris. May he not be rejected, may he not be turned back, may he enter in [as he] pleaseth, may he come forth [as he] desireth, and may he be victorious. May his bidding be done in the house of Osiris; may he walk, and may he speak with you, and may he be a glorified soul along with you. He hath not been found wanting there, and the Balance is rid of [his] trial."

Appendix: After the First Chapter M. Naville has printed in his *Todtenbuch* the text of a composition which also refers to the funeral, and which he has designated Chapter 1B. It is entitled "Chapter of making the mummy to go into the underworld on the day of the funeral." The text is, however, mutilated in places; and the following version has been made by the help of the two copies of the text published by Pleyte, *Chapitres Supplémentaires au Livre des Morts*, p. 182 ff.; and by Birch, *Proc. Soc. Bibl. Arch.*, 1885, p. 84 f.

"Homage to thee, O thou who livest in Set-Sert of Amenta. Osiris the scribe Nekht-Amen, triumphant, knoweth thy name. Deliver thou him from the worms which are in Re-stau, and which feed upon the bodies of men and drink their blood. Osiris, the favoured one of his divine city, the royal scribe Nekht-Amen, triumphant, is known unto you [ye worms] and he knoweth your names. This is the first bidding of Osiris, the Lord of All, who hath completed all his hidden works: 'Give thou breath [unto them] who fear those who are in the Bight of the Stream of Amenta.' He hath ordered the plans of His throne is placed within the darkness, and there is given unto him glory in Re-stau. O god of light, come thou down unto me and swallow up the worms which are in Amenta, The great god who dwelleth within Tattu, whom he seeth not, heareth his prayers. They who are in affliction fear him [the god] who cometh forth with the sentence at the sacred block. Osiris, the royal scribe Nekht-Amen, cometh with the decree of the Lord of All, and Horus hath taken possession of his throne for him. He cometh with tidings; [may he enter in] according to his word and may he see Annu. The nobles have stood up on the ground before him, and the scribes magnify him. The princes bind his swathings, and make festivals for him in Annu. For him hath heaven been led captive; he hath seized the inheritance of the earth in his grasp. Neither heaven nor earth can be taken away from him, for, behold, he is Ra, the first-born of the gods. His mother suckleth him, she giveth her breast from the sky."

Rubric: The words of this chapter are to be said after [the deceased] is laid to rest in Amenta, etc.

CHAPTER OF GIVING A MOUTH TO OSIRIS ANI, THE SCRIBE AND TELLER OF THE HOLY OFFERINGS OF ALL THE GODS. MAY HE BE VICTORIOUS IN NETER-KHERT! "I rise out of the egg in the hidden land. May my mouth be given unto me that I may speak with it before the great god, the lord of the underworld. May my hand and my arm not be forced back by the holy ministers of any god. I am Osiris, the lord of the mouth of the tomb; and Osiris, the victorious scribe Ani, hath a portion 3 with him who is upon the top of the steps. According to the desire of my heart, I have come from the Pool of Fire, and I have quenched it. Homage to thee, O thou lord of brightness, thou who art at the head of the Great House, and who dwellest in night and in thick darkness; I have come unto thee. I am glorious, I am pure; my arms support thee. Thy portion shall be with those who have gone before. O grant unto me my mouth that I may speak therewith; and that I may follow my heart when it passeth through the fire and darkness."

RUBRIC: If this writing be known [by the deceased] upon earth, and this chapter be done into writing upon [his] coffin, he shall come forth by day in all the forms of existence which he desireth, and he shall enter into [his] place and shall not be rejected. Bread and ale and meat shall be given unto Osiris, the scribe Ani, upon the altar of Osiris. He shall enter into the Fields of Aaru in peace, to learn the bidding of him who dwelleth in Tattu; there shall wheat and barley be given unto him; there shall he flourish as he did upon earth; and he shall do whatsoever pleaseth him, even as [do] the gods who are in the underworld, for everlasting millions of ages, world without end.

Appendix: The text of Chapter LXXII. does not occur in the Papyrus of Ani. It is given by M. Naville (see *Todtenbuch*, I., Bl. 84) from, a papyrus in the Louvre. In the vignettes which accompany it, the deceased is represented as adoring three gods, who are either standing in a shrine or are seated upon it. In other instances, the deceased stands by a sepulchral chest or outside a pylon with hands raised in adoration. The following is a translation of the Louvre text:—

CHAPTER OF COMING FORTH BY DAY AND OF PASSING THROUGH THE AMMAHET. "Homage to you, O ye lords of *kas*, ye lords of right and truth, infallible, who shall endure for ever and shall exist through countless ages, grant that 1 may enter into your [presence]. I, even I, am pure and holy, and I have gotten power over the spells which are mine. judgment hath been passed upon me in my glorified form. Deliver ye me from the crocodile which is in the place of the lords of right and truth. Grant ye unto me my mouth that I may speak therewith. May offerings be made unto me in your presence, for I know you and I know your names, and I know the name of the great god. Grant ye abundance of food for his nostrils. The god Rekem passeth through the western horizon of heaven. He travelleth on, and I travel on he goeth forth, and I go forth. Let me not be destroyed in the place Mesqet let not the Fiend get the mastery over me; let me not be driven back from your gates; let not your doors be shut against me; for I have [eaten] bread in Pe and I have drunken ale in Tepu. If my arms be fettered in the holy habitation, may my father Tmu stablish for me my mansion in the place above [this] earth where there are wheat and barley in abundance which cannot be told. May feasts be made for me there, for my soul and for my body. Grant me even offerings of the dead, bread, and ale, and wine, oxen, and ducks, linen bandages and incense, wax, and all the good and fair and pure things whereby the gods do live. May I rise again in all the forms which I desire without fail and for ever. May I sail up and down through the fields of Aaru; may I come thither in peace; for I am the double Lion-god."

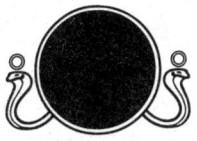

PLATE

7

Vignette: The vignette of these plates, forming one composition, runs along the top of the text. The subjects are:-

PLATE 7

1. Ani and his wife in the *seh* hall; he is moving a piece on a draught-board.
2. The souls of Ani and his wife standing upon a pylon-shaped building. The hieroglyphics by the side of Ani's soul read *ba en Ausar*, "the soul of Osiris."
3. A table of offerings, upon which are laid a libation vase, plants, and lotus flowers.
4. Two lions seated back to back and supporting the horizon, over which extends the sky. The lion on the right is called *Sef*, *i.e.*, "Yesterday," and that on the left *Tuau*, *i.e.*, "Tomorrow".
5. The *bennu* bird, and a table of offerings.

6. The mummy of Ani lying on a bier within a funereal shrine; the head and foot are Nephthys and Isis in the form of hawks. Beneath the bier are vases painted to imitate variegated marble or glass, a funereal box, Ani's palette, etc.

PLATE 8

1. The god Heh "Millions of years," wearing the emblem of "years" (upon his head, and holding a similar object in his right hand; he is kneeling and extends his left hand over a pool in which is an eye.
2. The god *Uatch-ura*, "Great Green Water," with each hand extended over a pool; that under his right hand is called *She en hesmen*, "Pool of Natron," and that under his left hand *She en Maaat*, "Pool of Nitre *or* Salt".
3. A pylon with doors, called *Re-stau*, "Gate of the funereal passages".
4. The *utchat* facing to the left above a pylon.
5. The cow (Fig. 1) *Mehurt maat Ra*, "Mehurt, the eye of Ra," with a flail and having on her head a disk and horns and round her neck the collar and menat.

FIG. I.

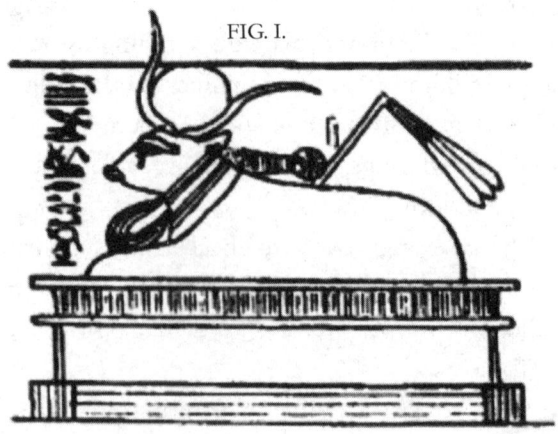

PLATE 7

6. A funereal chest from which emerge the head of Ra, and his two arms and hands, each holding the emblem of life. The chest, which is called *aat Abtu*, "the district of Abydos," or the "burial place of the East," has upon its side figures of the four children of Horus who protect the intestines of Osiris or the deceased. On the right stand Tuamautef and Qebhsennuf, and on the left Mestha and Hapi.

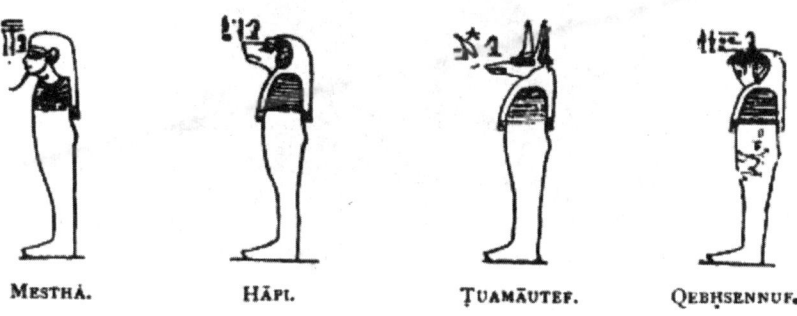

MESTHÀ. HÀPI. ṬUAMĀUTEF. QEBHSENNUF.

PLATE 9

1. Figures of three gods who, together with Mestha, Hapi, Tuamautef, and Qebhsennuf, are the "seven shining ones". Their names are: Maa-atef-f, Kheri-beq-f, and Heru-khent-maati.
2. The god Anpu (Anubis), jackal-headed.
3. Figures of seven gods, whose names are Netchehnetcheh, Aaqetqet, Khenti-heh-f, Ami-unnut-f, Tesher-maa,, Bes-maa-em-kerh, and An-em-hru.
4. The soul of Ra, and the soul of Osiris in the form of a human-headed bird wearing the crown conversing in Tattu a scene of very rare occurrence.

PLATE 10

1. The Cat, *i.e.*, the Sun, which dwelleth by the persea tree in Heliopolis, cutting off the head of the serpent Apepi, emblematic of his enemies.
2. Three seated deities holding knives. They are probably Sau, Horus of Sekhem, and Nefer-Tmu.
3. Ani and his wife Thuthu, who holds a sistrum, kneeling in adoration before the god Khepera, beetle-headed, who is seated in the boat of the rising sun.
4. Two apes, emblematic of Isis and Nephthys.
5. The god Tmu, seated within the Sun-disk in the boat of the setting sun, facing a table of offerings.
6. The god Rehu, in the form of a lion.
7. The serpent Uatchit, the lady of flame, a symbol of the eye of Ra, coiled round a lotus flower. Above is the emblem of fire.

PLATE 7

TEXT FOR PLATES 7-10

HERE BEGIN THE PRAISES AND GLORIFYINGS OF
COMING OUT FROM AND GOING INTO THE GLORIOUS
NETER-KHERT IN THE BEAUTIFUL AMENTA, OF COMING OUT
BY DAY IN ALL THE FORMS OF EXISTENCE WHICH PLEASE
HIM (i.e., THE DECEASED), OF PLAYING AT DRAUGHTS' AND
SITTING IN THE SEH HALL, AND OF COMING FORTH AS A
LIVING SOUL.

Behold Osiris, the scribe Ani, after he hath come to his haven
[of rest]. That which hath been done upon earth [by Ani] being
blessed, all the words of the god Tmu come to pass. "I am the
god Tmu in [my] rising; I am the only One. I came into existence
in Nu. I am Ra who rose in the beginning. [He hath ruled that
which he made.]"

Who then is this? It is Ra who rose for the first time in the
city of Suten-henen [crowned] as a king in [his] rising. The pillars
of Shu were not as yet created, when he was upon the high place
of him who is in Khemennu." I am the great god who gave birth
to himself, even Nu, [who] created his name *Paut Neteru* as god."

Who then is this? It is Ra, the creator of the name[s] of his
limbs, which came into being in the form of the gods in the train
of Ra.

"I am he who is not driven back among the gods."

Who then is this? It is Tmu in his disk, or (as others say), It is
Ra in his rising in the eastern horizon of heaven.

"I am Yesterday; I know Tomorrow."

Who then is this? Yesterday is Osiris, and Tomorrow is Ra,
on the day when he shall destroy the enemies of Neb-er-tcher,
and when he shall stablish as prince and ruler his son Horus, or
(as others say), on the day when we commemorate the festival of
the meeting of the dead Osiris with his father Ra, and when the

battle of the gods was fought in which Osiris, lord of Amentet, was the leader.

What then is this? It is Amentet, [that is to say] the creation of the souls of the gods when Osiris was leader in Set-Amentet; or (as others say), Amentet is that which Ra hath given unto me; when any god cometh, he doth arise and doeth battle for it.

"I know the god who dwelleth therein."

Who then is this? It is Osiris," or (as others say), Ra is his name, even Ra the self-created.

"I am the *bennu* bird which is in Annu, and I am the keeper of the volume of the book of things which are and of things which shall be."

Who then is this? It is Osiris, or (as others say), It is his dead body, or (as others say), It is his filth. The things which are are and the things which shall be are his dead body; or (as others say), They are eternity and everlastingness. Eternity is the day, and everlastingness is the night.

"I am the god Amsu in his coming-forth; may his two plumes be set upon my head."

Who then is this? Amsu is Horus, the avenger of his father, and his coming-forth is his birth. The plumes upon his head are Isis and Nephthys when they go forth to set themselves there, even as his protectors, and they provide that which his head lacketh, or (as others say), They are the two exceeding great uraei which are upon the head of their father Tmu, or (as others say), His two eyes are the two plumes. "Osiris Ani, the scribe of all the holy offerings, riseth up in his place in triumph; he cometh into his city." What then is this? It is the horizon of his father Tmu. "1 have made an end of my shortcomings, and I have put away my faults." What then is this? It is the cutting off of the corruptible in the body of Osiris, the scribe Ani, triumphant before all the gods; and all his faults are driven out. What then is this? It is the

PLATE 7

purification [of Osiris] on the day of his birth. "I am purified in my exceeding great double nest which is in Suten henen, on the day of the offerings of the followers of the great god who is therein." What then is this? "Millions of years" is the name of the one [nest], "Green Lake" is the name of the other; a pool of natron, and a pool of nitre ; or (as others say), "The Traverser of Millions of Years" is the name of the one, "Great Green Lake" is the name of the other; or (as others say), "The Begetter of Millions of Years" is the name of the one, "Green Lake" is the name of the other. Now as concerning the great god who is in it, it is Ra himself. "I pass over the way, I know the head of the Pool of Maata." What then is this? It is Re-stau; that is to say, it is the underworld on the south of Naarut-f, and it is the northern door of the tomb.

Now as concerning She-Maaat, it is Abtu; or (as others say), It is the road by which his father Tmu travelleth when he goeth to Sekhet-Aaru, which bringeth forth the food and nourishment of the gods behind the shrine. Now the Gate of Sert is the gate of the pillars of Shu, the northern gate of the underworld; or (as others say), It is the two leaves of the door through which the god Tmu passeth when he goeth forth in the eastern horizon of heaven.

"O ye gods who are in the presence (of Osiris), grant me your arms, for I am the god who shall come into being among you."

What then is this? It is the drops of blood which fell from Ra when he went forth to cut himself. They sprang into being as the gods Hu and Sa, who are in the following of Ra and who accompany Tmu daily and every day.

"I, Osiris, Ani the scribe, triumphant, have filled up for thee the *utchat* after it was darkened on the day of the combat of the Two Fighters."

What then is this? It is the day on which Horus fought with Set, who cast filth in the face of Horus, and when Horus destroyed the powers of Set. Thoth did this with his own hand.

"I lift the hair[-cloud] when there are storms in the sky."

What then is this? It is the right eye of Ra, which raged against [Set] when he sent it forth. Thoth raiseth up the hair[-cloud], and bringeth the eye alive, and whole, and sound, and without defect to [its] lord; or (as others say), It is the eye of Ra when it is sick and when it weepeth for its fellow eye; then Thoth standeth up to cleanse it.

"I behold Ra who was born yesterday from the buttocks of the cow Meh-urt; his strength is my strength, and my strength is his strength."

What then is this? It is the water of heaven, or (as others say), It is the image of the eye of Ra in the morning at his daily birth. Meh-urt is the eye of Ra. Therefore Osiris, the scribe Ani, triumphant, [is] a great one among the gods who are in the train of Horus. The words are] spoken for him that loveth his lord.

What then is this? [i.e., who are these gods?] Mestha, Hapi Tuamautef, and Qebhsennuf.

"Homage to you, O ye lords of right and truth, and ye holy ones who [stand] behind Osiris, who utterly do away with sins and crime, and [ye] who are in the following of the goddess Hetep-se-khus, grant that I may come unto you. Destroy ye all the faults which are within me, even as ye did for the seven Shining Ones who are among the followers of their lord Sepa. Anubis appointed their place on the day [when was said], 'Come therefore thither.'"

What then is this? These lords of right and truth are Thoth and Astes, lord of Amenta. The holy ones who stand behind Osiris, even Mestha, Hapi, Tuamautef, and Qebhsennuf, are they who are behind the Thigh in the northern sky. They who do away with sins and crime and who are in the following of the goddess

PLATE 7

Hetep-se-khus are the god Sebek in the waters. The goddess Hetep-se-khus is the eye of Ra, or (as others say), It is the flame which followeth after Osiris to burn up the souls of his foes. As concerning all the faults which are in Osiris, the scribe of the holy offerings of all the gods, Ani, triumphant, [they are all that he hath done against the lords of eternity] since he came forth from his mother's womb. As concerning the seven Shining Ones, even Mestha, Hapi, Tuamautef, Qebhsennuf, Maa-atef-f, Kheri-beq-f, and Horus-Khenti-maa, Anubis appointed them protectors of the body of Osiris, or (as others say), [set them] behind the place of purification of Osiris; or (as others say), Those seven glorious ones are Netcheh-netcheh, Aqet-qet, An-erta-nef-bes-f-khenti-heh-f, Aq-her-unnut-f, Tesher-maa-ammi -het-Anes, Ubes-hra-per-em-khet khet,[l] and Maa -em-qerh-an-nef-em-hru. The chief of the holy ones who minister in his chamber is Horus, the avenger of his father. As to the day [upon which was said] "Come therefore thither," it concerneth the words, "Come then thither," which Ra spake unto Osiris. Lo, may this be decreed for me in Amentet.

"I am the soul which dwelleth in the two *tchafi*."

What then is this? It is Osiris [when] he goeth into Tattu and findeth there the soul of Ra; there the one god embraceth the other, and souls spring into being within the two *tchafi*. ["I am the Cat which fought (?) by the Persea tree hard by in Annu, on the night when the foes of Neb-er-tcher were destroyed."]

What then is this? The male cat is Ra himself, and he is called Maau by reason of the speech of the god Sa [who said] concerning him: "He is like (*maau*) unto that which he hath made, and his name became Maau"; or (as others say), It is Shu who maketh over the possessions of Seb to Osiris. As to the fight (?) by the Persea tree hard by, in Annu, it concerneth the children of impotent revolt when justice is wrought on them for what they have done. As to [the words] "that night of the battle," they concern the inroad [of the children of impotent revolt] into the eastern part of heaven, whereupon there arose a battle in heaven and in all the earth.

"O thou who art in the egg (i.e., Ra), who shinest from thy disk and risest in thy horizon, and dost shine like gold above the sky, like unto whom there is none among the gods, who sailest over the pillars of Shu (*i.e.*, the ether), who givest blasts of fire from thy mouth, [who makest the two lands bright with thy radiance, deliver] the faithful worshippers from the god whose forms are hidden, whose eyebrows are like unto the two arms of the balance on the night of the reckoning of destruction."

Who then is this? It is An-a-f, the god who bringeth his arm. As concerning [the words] "that night of the reckoning of destruction," it is the night of the burning of the damned, and of the overthrow of the wicked at [the sacred] block, and of the slaughter of souls.

Who then is this? It is Nemu, the headsman of Osiris; or (as others say), It is Apep when he riseth up with one head bearing *maat* (*i.e.*, right and truth) [upon it]; or (as others say), It is Horus when he riseth up with two heads, whereof the one beareth *maat* and the other wickedness. He bestoweth wickedness on him that worketh wickedness, and *maat* on him that followeth after righteousness and truth; or (as others say), It is the great Horus who dwelleth in [Se] khem; or (as others say), It is Thoth; or (as others say), It is Nefer-Tmu, [or] Sept, who doth thwart the course of the foes of Neb-er-tcher.

"Deliver me from the Watchers who bear slaughtering knives, and who have cruel fingers, and who slay those who are in the following of Osiris. May they never overcome me, may I never fall under their knives."

"What then is this? It is Anubis, and it is Horus in the form of Khent-en-maa; or (as others say), It is the Divine Rulers who

PLATE 7

thwart the works of their [weapons]; it is the chiefs of the *sheniu* chamber.

"May their knives never get the mastery over me, may I never fall under their instruments of cruelty, for I know their names, and I know the being Matchet Who is among them in the house of Osiris, shooting rays of light from [his] eye, but he himself is unseen. He goeth round about heaven robed in the flame of his mouth, commanding Hapi, but remaining himself unseen. May I be strong upon earth before Ra, may I come happily into haven in the presence of Osiris. Let not your offerings be hurtful to me, O ye who preside over your altars, for I am among those who follow after Neb-er-tcher according to the writings of Khepera. I fly as a hawk, I cackle as a goose; I ever slay, even as the serpent goddess Nehebka."

What then is this? They who preside at the altars are the similitude of the eye of Ra and the similitude of the eye of Horus.

"O Ra-Tmu, lord of the Great House, prince, life, strength and health of all the gods, deliver thou [me] from the god whose face is like unto that of a dog, whose brows are as those of a man, and who feedeth upon the dead, who watcheth at the Bight of the Fiery Lake, and who devoureth the bodies of the dead and swalloweth hearts, and who shooteth forth filth, but he himself remaineth unseen."

Who then is this? "Devourer for millions of years" is his name, and he dwelleth in the Lake of Unt. As concerning the Fiery Lake, it is that which is in Anrutf, hard by the *Shenit* chamber. The unclean man who would walk thereover doth fall down among the knives; or (as others say), His name is "Mathes," and he is the watcher of the door of Amenta; or (as others say), His name is "Heri-sep-f."

"Hail, Lord of terror, chief of the lands of the North and South, lord of the red glow, who preparest the slaughter-block, and who dost feed upon the inward parts!"

Who then is this? The guardian of the Bight of Amenta.

What then is this? It is the heart of Osiris, which is the devourer of all slaughtered things. The *urerit* crown hath been given unto him with swellings of the heart as lord of Suten-henen.

What then is this? He to whom hath been given the *urerit* crown with swellings of-the heart as lord of Suten-henen is Osiris. He was bidden to rule among the gods on the day of the union of earth with earth in the presence of Neb-er-tcher.

What then is this? He that was bidden to rule among the gods is [Horus] the son of Isis, who was appointed to rule in the place of his father Osiris. As to the day of the union of earth with earth, it is the mingling of earth with earth in the coffin of Osiris, the Soul that liveth in Suten-henen, the giver of meat and drink, the destroyer of wrong, and the guide of the everlasting paths.

Who then is this? It is Ra himself.

"Deliver thou [me] from the great god who carrieth away souls, and who devoureth filth and eateth dirt, the guardian of the darkness [who himself liveth] in the light. They who are in misery fear him."

As concerning the souls within the *tchafi* [they are those which are] with the god who carrieth away the soul, who eateth hearts, and who feedeth upon offal, the guardian of the darkness who is within the *seker* boat; they who live in crime fear him.

Who then is this? It is Suti, or (as others say), It is Smam-ur, the soul of Seb.

"Hail, Khepera in thy boat, the twofold company of the gods is thy body. Deliver thou Osiris Ani, triumphant, from the watchers who give judgment, who have been appointed by Neb-er-tcher to protect him and to fasten the fetters on his foes, and who slaughter in the shambles; there is no escape from their grasp. May they never stab me with their knives, may I never fall helpless in their chambers of torture. Never have the things which the gods hate been done

PLATE 7

by me, for I am pure within the Mesqet. Cakes of saffron have been brought unto him in Tanenet."

Who then is this? It is Khepera in his boat. It is Ra himself. The watchers who give judgment are the apes Isis and Nephthys. The things which the gods hate are wickedness and falsehood; and he who passeth through the place of purification within the Mesqet is Anubis, who is behind the chest which holdeth the inward parts of Osiris.

He to whom saffron cakes have been brought in Tanenet is Osiris; or (as others say), The saffron cakes in Tanenet are heaven and earth, or (as others say), They are Shu, strengthener of the two lands in Suten-henen. The saffron cakes are the eye of Horus; and Tanenet is the grave of Osiris.

Tmu hath built thy house, and the two-fold Lion-god hath founded thy habitation; lo! drugs are brought, and Horus purifieth and Set strengtheneth, and Set purifieth and Horus strengtheneth.

"The Osiris, the scribe Ani, triumphant before Osiris, hath come into the land, and hath possessed it with his feet. He is Tmu, and he is in the city."

"Turn thou back, O Rehu, whose mouth shineth, whose head moveth, turn thou back from before his strength"; or (as others say), Turn thou back from him who keepeth watch and is unseen. "The Osiris Ani is safely guarded. He is Isis, and he is found with [her] hair spread over him. I shake it out over his brow. He was conceived in Isis and begotten in Nephthys; and they cut off from him the things which should be cut off."

Fear followeth after thee, terror is upon thine arms. Thou art embraced for millions of years in the arms [of the nations]; mortals go round about thee. Thou smitest down the mediators of thy foes, and thou seizest the arms of the powers of darkness. The two sisters (i.e., Isis and Nephthys) are given to thee for thy delight. Thou hast created that which is in Kheraba, and that which is in Annu. Every god feareth thee, for thou art exceeding great and terrible; thou [avengest] every god on the man that curseth him, and thou shootest out arrows Thou livest according to thy will; thou art Uatchit, the Lady of Flame. Evil cometh among those who set themselves up against thee.

What then is this? The hidden in form, granted of Menhu, is the name of the tomb. He seeth [what is] in [his] hand, is the name of the shrine, or (as others say), the name of the block. Now he whose mouth shineth and whose head moveth is a limb of Osiris, or (as others say), of Ra. Thou spreadest thy hair and I shake it out over his brow is spoken concerning Isis, who hideth in her hair and draweth her hair over her. Uatchi, the Lady of Flames, is the eye of Ra.

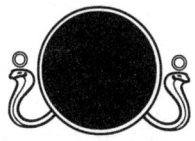

PLATES

11–12

Vignette I.: Ani and his wife Thuthu approaching the first Arit, the cornice of which is ornamented with *i.e.,* emblems of power, life, and stability. At the entrance sit three gods, the first having the head of a hare, the second the head of a serpent, and the third the head of a crocodile. The first holds an ear of corn (?), and each of the others a knife.

THE FIRST ARIT. The name of the doorkeeper is Sekhet-hra-asht-aru; the name of the watcher is Meti-heh; the name of the herald is Ha-kheru.

[WORDS TO BE SPOKEN WHEN OSIRIS COMETH TO THE FIRST ARIT IN AMENTA.] Saith Ani, triumphant, when he cometh to the first Arit: "I am the mighty one who createth his own light.

I have come unto thee, O Osiris, and, purified from that which defileth thee, I adore thee. Lead on; name not the name of Re-stau unto me. Homage to thee, O Osiris, in thy might and in thy strength in Re-stau. Rise up and conquer, O Osiris, in Abtu. Thou goest round about heaven, thou sailest in the presence of Ra, thou seest all the beings who have knowledge. Hail Ra, who circlest in [the sky]. Verily I say [unto thee], O Osiris, I am a godlike ruler. Let me not be driven hence nor from the wall of burning coals. [I have] opened the way in Re-stau; I have eased the pain of Osiris; [I have] embraced that which the balance I hath weighed; [I have] made a path for him in the great valley, it and [he] maketh a path. Osiris shineth(?)."

Vignette II.: The second Arit, guarded by three gods; the first of whom has the head of a lion, the second the head of a man, and the third the head of a dog. Each one holds a knife.

THE SECOND ARIT. The name of the doorkeeper is Un-hat; the name of the watcher is Seqet-hra; the name of the herald is Uset.

Saith Osiris Ani, when he cometh unto this Arit; "He sitteth to do his heart's desire, and he weigheth words as the second of Thoth. The strength of Thoth humbleth the hidden Maata gods who feed upon Maat throughout the years [of their lives]. I make offerings at the moment when [he] passeth on his way; I pass on and enter on the way; Grant thou that I may pass through and that I may gain sight of Ra together with those who make offerings."

Vignette III.: The third Arit, guarded by three gods; the first with the head of a jackal, the second the head of a dog, and the third the head of a serpent. The first holds an ear of corn (?), and each of the others a knife.

THE THIRD ARIT. The name of the doorkeeper is Qeq-hauau-ent-pehui; the name of the watcher is Se-res-hra; the name of the herald is Aaa.

Saith Osiris Ani, [when he cometh to this Arit]: "I am hidden [in] the great deep, [I am] the judge of the Rehui. I have come and

PLATE 11-12: PYLONS

Vignette I.: Ani and his wife Thuthu, with hands raised in adoration, approaching the first *Sebkhet* or Pylon, which is guarded by a bird-headed deity wearing a disk on his head, and sitting in a shrine the cornice of which is decorated with *khakeru* ornaments.

THE FIRST PYLON. WORDS TO BE SPOKEN WHEN [ANI] COMETH UNTO THE FIRST PYLON. Saith Osiris Ani, triumphant: "Lo, the lady of terrors, with lofty walls, the sovereign lady, the mistress of destruction, who uttereth the words which drive back the destroyers, who delivereth from destruction him that travelleth along the way. The name of the doorkeeper is Neruit."

Vignette II.: The second Pylon, which is guarded by a lion-headed deity seated in a shrine, upon the top of which is a serpent.

WORDS TO BE SPOKEN WHEN [ANI] COMETH UNTO THE SECOND PYLON. Saith Osiris, the scribe Ani, triumphant: "Lo, the lady of heaven, the mistress of the world, who devoureth with fire, the lady of mortals; how much greater is she than all men! The name of the doorkeeper is Mes-Ptah."

Vignette III.: The third Pylon, which is guarded by a man-headed deity seated in a shrine, the upper part of which is ornamented with the two *utchats* and the emblems of the orbit of the sun and of water.

WORDS TO BE SPOKEN WHEN [ANI] COMETH UNTO THE THIRD PYLON OF THE HOUSE OF OSIRIS. Saith the scribe Ani, triumphant: "Lo, the lady of the altar, the mighty one to whom offerings are made, the beloved (?) of every god, who saileth up to Abtu. The name of the doorkeeper is Sebaq."

Vignette IV.: The fourth Pylon, which is guarded by a cow-headed deity seated in a shrine, the cornice of which is ornamented with uraei wearing disks.

WORDS TO BE SPOKEN WHEN [ANI] COMETH UNTO THE FOURTH PYLON. Saith Osiris, the scribe Ani, [triumphant]: "Lo, she who prevaileth with knives, mistress of the world, destroyer of the foes of the Still-Heart, she who decreeth the escape of the needy from evil hap. The name of the doorkeeper is Nekau."

Vignette V.: The fifth Pylon, which is guarded by the hippopotamus deity, with her fore-feet resting upon the buckle, the emblem of protection, seated in a shrine, the cornice of which is ornamented with emblematic of flames of fire.

WORDS TO BE SPOKEN WHEN [ANI] COMETH UNTO THE FIFTH PYLON. Saith Osiris, the scribe Ani, triumphant: "Lo, the flame, the lady of breath (?) for the nostrils; one may not advance to entreat her shall not come into her presence. The name of the doorkeeper is Hentet-Arqiu."

Vignette VI.: The sixth Pylon, which is guarded by a deity in the form of a man holding a knife and a besom and seated in a shrine, above which is a serpent.

WORDS TO BE SPOKEN WHEN [ANI] COMETH UNTO THE SIXTH PYLON. Saith Osiris, the scribe Ani, triumphant: "Lo, the lady of light, the mighty one, to whom men cry aloud; man knoweth neither her breadth nor her height; there was never found her like from the beginning (?). There is a serpent thereover whose size is not known; it was born in the presence of the Still-Heart. The name of the doorkeeper is Semati."

Vignette VII.: The seventh Pylon, which is guarded by a ram-headed deity holding a besom and seated in a shrine, the cornice of which is decorated with *khakeru* ornaments.

WORDS TO BE SPOKEN WHEN [ANI] COMETH UNTO THE SEVENTH PYLON. Saith Osiris, the scribe Ani, triumphant: "Lo, the robe which doth clothe the feeble one (*i.e.*, the deceased), weeping for what it loveth and shroudeth. The name of the doorkeeper is Sakti-f."

Vignette VIII.: The eighth Pylon, which is guarded by a hawk wearing the crowns of the North and South, seated on a sepulchral chest with closed doors; before him is a besom, and behind him is the *utchat*. Above the shrine are two human-headed hawks, emblems of the souls of Ra and Osiris, and two emblems of life.

WORDS TO BE SPOKEN WHEN [ANI] COMETH UNTO THE EIGHTH PYLON. Saith Osiris, the scribe Ani, triumphant: "Lo, the blazing fire, the flame whereof cannot be quenched, with tongues of flame which reach afar, the slaughtering one, the irresistible, through which one may not pass by reason of the hurt which it doeth. The name of the doorkeeper is Khu-tchet-f."

Vignette IX: The ninth Pylon, which is guarded by a lion-headed deity wearing a disk and holding a besom, seated in a shrine, the cornice of which is ornamented with uraei wearing disks.

WORDS TO BE SPOKEN WHEN [ANI] COMETH UNTO THE NINTH PYLON. Saith Osiris Ani, triumphant: "Lo, she who is chiefest, the lady of strength, who giveth quiet of heart to her lord. Her girth is three hundred and fifty measures; she is clothed with mother-of-emerald of the south; and she raiseth up the godlike form and clotheth the feeble one The name of the doorkeeper is Ari-su-tchesef."

Vignette X.: The tenth Pylon, which is guarded by a ram-headed deity wearing the *atef* crown and holding a besom, seated in a shrine, upon the top of which are two serpents.

WORDS TO BE SPOKEN WHEN [ANI] COMETH UNTO THE TENTH PYLON. Saith Osiris Ani, [triumphant]: "Lo, she who is loud of voice, she who causeth those to cry who entreat her, the fearful one who terrifieth, who feareth none that are therein. The name of the doorkeeper is Sekhen-ur."

Appendix: The several "texts" of the next eleven Pylons are wanting in this papyrus. Translations of them are here given as they are found in a papyrus published by Naville, *Todtenbuch*, Bd. I., 131. 161, 162. It will be observed that the names of the doorkeepers are wanting, and also that each text, except in the case of the twenty-first Pylon, ends with words which refer to the examination of the dead at each gate.

THE ELEVENTH PYLON. "Lo, she who repeateth slaughter, the burner up of fiends, It she who is terrible at every gateway, who rejoiceth on the day of darkness. She judgeth the feeble swathed one."

THE TWELFTH PYLON. "Lo, the invoker of the two lands, who destroyeth with flashings and with fire those who come, the lady of splendour, who obeyeth her lord daily. She judgeth the feeble swathed one."

THE THIRTEENTH PYLON. "Lo, Isis, who hath stretched forth her hands and arms over it, and hath made Hapi to shine in his hidden place. She judgeth the feeble swathed one."

THE FOURTEENTH PYLON. "Lo, the lady of the knife, who danceth in blood; she maketh [the festival of] the god Hak on the day of judgment. She judgeth the feeble swathed one."

THE FIFTEENTH PYLON. "Lo, the Bloody Soul, who searcheth out and putteth to the test, who maketh inquiry and scrutiny, who cometh forth by night, and doth fetter the Fiend in his lair; may her hands be given to the Still-Heart in his hour, and may she make him to advance and come forth unto her. She judgeth the feeble swathed one."

THE SIXTEENTH PYLON. Saith Osiris, when he cometh unto this pylon: "Lo, the Terrible one, the lady of the rain storm, who planteth ruin in the souls of men, the devourer of the dead bodies of mankind, the orderer and creator of slaughters, who cometh forth. She judgeth the feeble swathed one."

THE SEVENTEENTH PYLON. "Lo, the Hewer-in-pieces in blood, the lady of flame. She judgeth the feeble swathed one."

THE EIGHTEENTH PYLON. "Lo, the Lover of fire, the purifier of sinners the lover of slaughter, the chief of those who adore, the lady of the temple, the slaughterer of the fiends in the night. She judgeth the feeble bandaged one."

THE NINETEENTH PYLON. "Lo, the Dispenser of light while she liveth, the mistress of flames, the lady of the strength and of the writings of Ptah himself. She maketh trial of the swathings of Pa-an."

THE TWENTIETH PYLON. "Lo, she who is within the cavern of her lord, Clother is her name; she hideth what she hath made, she carrieth away hearts and greedily drinketh water. She judgeth the feeble swathed one."

THE TWENTY-FIRST PYLON. "Lo, the knife which cutteth when [its name] is uttered, and slayeth those who advance towards its flames. It hath secret plots and counsels."

In the late recensions of the Book of the Dead, the text referring to the twenty-first Pylon reads:—

"Hail," saith Horus, "O twenty-first pylon of the Still-Heart. I have made the way, I know thee, I know thy name, I know the name of the goddess who guardeth thee: 'Sword that smiteth at the utterance of its [own] name, the unknown (?) goddess with back-turned face, the overthrower of those who draw nigh unto her flame' is her name. Thou keepest the secret things of the avenger of the god whom thou guardest, and his name is Amem. He maketh it to come to pass that the persea trees grow not, that the acacia trees bring not forth, and that copper is not begotten in the mountain. The godlike beings of this pylon are seven gods. Tchen or At is the name of the one at (?) the door; Hetep-mes is the name of the second one; Mes-Sep is the name of the third one Utch-re is the name of the fourth one; "Ap-uat is the name of the fifth one; Beq is the name of the sixth one; Anubis is the name of the seventh one."

"I have made the way. I am Amsu-Horus, the avenger of his father, the heir of his father Un-nefer. I have come and I have overthrown all foes of my father Osiris. I have come day by day with victory, doing myself the worship of the god, (76) in the house of his father Tmu, lord of Annu, triumphant in the southern sky. I have done what is right and true to him that hath made right and truth; I have made the Haker festival for the lord thereof; I have led the way in the festival; I have made offerings of cakes to the lords of the altars; and I have brought offerings and oblations, and cakes and ale, and oxen and ducks, to my father Osiris Un-nefer. I rise up in order that my soul may be made one wholly; I cause the bennu bird to come forth at [my] words. I have come daily into the holy house to make offerings of incense. I have brought garments of byssus. I have set forth on the lake in the boat. I have made Osiris, the overlord of the netherworld, to be victorious over his enemies; and I have carried away all his foes to the place of slaughter in the East; they shall never come forth from the durance of the god Seb therein. I have made those who stand up against Ra to be still, and [I have] made him to be victorious. I have come even as a scribe, and I have made all things plain. I have caused the god to have the power of his legs. I have come into the house of him that is upon his hill, and I have seen him that is ruler in the sacred hall. I have gone into Re-stau; I have hidden myself, and I have found out the way; I have travelled unto An-rutf. I have clothed those who are naked. I have sailed up to Abtu; I have praised the gods Hu and Sau. 1 have entered into the house of Astes, I have made supplication to the gods Khati and Sekhet in the house of Neith, "or, as others say," the rulers. I have entered into Re-stau; I have hidden myself, and I have found out the way; I have travelled unto An-rutf. I have clothed him who was naked. I have sailed up to Abtu; I have glorified Hu and Sau. I have received my crown at my rising, and I have power to sit upon my throne, upon the throne of my father and of the great company of the gods. I have adored the *meskhen* of Ta-sert. My mouth uttereth words with right and with truth. I have drowned the serpent Akhekh. I have come into the great hall which giveth strength unto the limbs; and it hath been granted to me to sail along in the boat of Hai. The fragrance of *anti* unguent ariseth from the hair of him who hath knowledge. I have entered into the house of Astes, and I have made supplication to the gods

Khati and Sekhet within the House of the Prince. I have arrived as a favoured one in Tattu."

Vignette [CHAPTER XVIII.—INTRODUCTION] (Upper register): The priest An-maut-f, who has on the right side of his head the lock of Heru-pa-khrat, or Horus the Child, and who wears a leopard's skin, introducing Ani and his wife to the gods whose names are given in Plates 13 and 14.

Text: An-maut-f saith: "I have come unto you, O mighty and godlike rulers who are in heaven and in earth and under the earth; and I have brought unto you Osiris Ani. He hath not sinned against any of the gods. Grant ye that he may be with you for all time."

The adoration of Osiris, lord of Re-stau, and of the great company of the gods who are in the netherworld beside Osiris, the scribe Ani, who saith: "Homage to thee, O ruler of Amenta, Unnefer within Abtu! I have come unto thee, and my heart holdeth right and truth. There is no sin in my body; nor have I lied wilfully, nor have I done aught with a false heart. Grant thou to me food in the tomb, and that I may come into [thy] presence at the altar of the lords of right and truth, and that I may enter into and come forth from the netherworld (my soul not being turned back), and that I may behold the face of the Sun, and that I may behold the Moon for ever and ever."

Vignette (Lower register): The priest Se-mer-f who has on the right side of his head the lock of Heru-pa-khrat and wears a leopard's skin, introducing Ani and his wife to the gods whose names are given in Plates 13 and 14.

Text: Se-mer-f saith I have come unto you, O godlike rulers who are in Re-stau, and I have brought unto you Osiris Ani. Grant ye [to him], as to the followers of Horus, cakes and water, and air, and a homestead in Sekhet-Hetep."

The adoration of Osiris, the lord of everlastingness, and of all the godlike rulers of Re-stau, by Osiris, [the scribe Ani], who saith: "Homage to thee, O king of Amenta, prince of Akert, I have come unto thee. I know thy ways, I am furnished with the forms which thou takest in the underworld. Grant thou to me a place in the underworld near unto the lords of right and truth. May my homestead be abiding in Sekhet-hetep, and may I receive cakes in thy presence."

PLATE

13

Vignettes (Upper register): A pylon, or gateway, surmounted by the feathers of Maat and uraei wearing disks. (Lower register): A pylon, surmounted by Anubis and an *utchat*.

"Hail Thoth, who madest Osiris victorious over his enemies, make thou Osiris [the scribe Ani] to be victorious over his enemies, as thou didst make Osiris victorious over his enemies' in the presence of the godlike rulers who are with Ra and Osiris in Annu, on the night of 'the things for the night,' and on the night of battle, and on the shackling of the fiends, and on the day of the destruction of Neb-er-tcher."]

§A. **Vignette:** The gods Tmu, Shut Tefnut, Osiris, and Thoth.

The great godlike rulers in Annu are Tmu, Shu, Tefnut [Osiris, and Thoth], and the shackling of the Sebau signifieth the destruction of the fiends of Set when he worketh evil a second time.

PLATE 13

"Hail, Thoth, who madest Osiris victorious over his enemies, make thou the Osiris Ani to be victorious over his enemies in the presence of the great divine beings who are in Tattu, on the night of making the Tat to stand up in Tattu."

§B. **Vignette:** The gods Osiris, Isis, Nephthys, and Horus.

The great godlike rulers in Tattu are Osiris, Isis, Nephthys, and Horus, the avenger of his father. Now the "night of making the Tat to stand Up in Tattu" signifieth [the lifting up of] the arm and shoulder of Osiris, lord of Sekhem; and these gods stand behind Osiris [to protect him] even as the swathings; which clothe him.

"Hail, Thoth, who madest Osiris victorious over his enemies, make thou the Osiris Ani triumphant over his enemies in the presence of the great godlike rulers who are in Sekhem, on the night of the things of the night [festival] in Sekhem."

§C. **Vignette:** The gods Osiris and Horus, two *utchats* upon pylons, and the god Thoth.

The great godlike rulers who are in Sekhem are Horus, who is without sight, and Thoth, who is with the godlike rulers in Naarerutf. Now the "night of the things of the night festival in Sekhem" signifieth the light of the rising sun on the coffin of Osiris.

"Hail, Thoth, who madest Osiris victorious over his enemies, make thou the Osiris Ani triumphant over his enemies in the presence of the great godlike rulers in Pe and Tep, on the night of setting up the columns of Horus, and of making him to be established the heir of the things which belonged to his father."

§D. **Vignette:** The gods Horus, Isis, Mestha and Hapi.

The great divine rulers who are in Pe and Tep are Horus, Isis, Mestha, and Hapi. Now setting up the columns of Horus [signifieth] the command given by Set unto his followers: "Set up columns upon it."

"Hail, Thoth, who madest Osiris victorious over his enemies, make thou the Osiris-Ani triumphant over his enemies in the presence of the great godlike it rulers in Rekhit, on the night when Isis lay down to keep watch in It order to make lamentation for her brother Osiris."

§E. **Vignette:** The gods Isis, Horus, Anubis, Mesthi, and Thoth.

The great godlike rulers who are in. Rekhit are Isis, Horus, and Mestha.

"Hail, Thoth, who madest Osiris victorious over his enemies, make thou the Osiris, the scribe Ani (triumphant in peace!), to be victorious over his enemies in the presence of the great godlike ones who are in Abtu, on the night of the god Naker, at the separation of the wicked dead, at the judgment of spirits made just, and at the arising of joy in Tenu."

PLATE

14

§F. Vignette: The gods Osiris, Isis, and Ap-uat, and the TET.

The great godlike rulers who are in Abtu are Osiris, Isis, and Ap-uat.

"Hail, Thoth, who madest Osiris victorious over his enemies, make thou the Osiris Ani, the scribe and teller of the sacred offerings of all the gods, to be victorious over his enemies in the presence of the godlike rulers who judge the dead, on the night of the condemnation of those who are to be blotted out."

§G. Vignette: The gods Thoth, Osiris, Anubis, and Astennu.

The great godlike rulers in the judgment of the dead are Thoth, Osiris, Anubis, and Astennu. Now the "condemnation of those who are to be blotted out" is the withholding of that which is so needful to the souls of the children of impotent revolt.

"Hail, Thoth, who madest Osiris victorious over his enemies, make thou the Osiris, the scribe Ani (triumphant!), to be victorious over his enemies in the presence of the great godlike rulers, on the festival of the breaking and turning up of the earth in Tattu, on the night of the breaking and turning up of the earth in their blood and of making Osiris to be victorious over his enemies."

§H. **Vignette:** The three gods of the festival of breaking up the earth in Tattu.

When the fiends of Set come and change themselves into beasts, the great godlike rulers, on the festival of the breaking and turning up of the earth in Tattu, slay them in the presence of the gods therein, and their blood floweth among them as they are smitten down. These things are allowed to be done by them by the judgment of those who are in Tattu.

"Hail, Thoth, who madest Osiris victorious over his enemies, make thou the Osiris Ani to be victorious over his enemies in the presence of the godlike rulers who are in Naarutef, on the night of him who concealeth himself in divers forms, even Osiris."

§I. **Vignette:** The gods Ra, Osiris, Shu, and Bebi, dog-headed.

The great godlike rulers who are in Naarutef are Ra, Osiris, Shu, and Bebi. Now the night of him who concealeth himself in divers forms, even Osiris," is when the thigh [and the head], and the heel, and the leg, are brought nigh unto the coffin of Osiris Un-nefer.

"Hail, Thoth, who madest Osiris victorious over his enemies, make thou the Osiris Ani (triumphant before Osiris) victorious over his enemies in the presence of the great godlike rulers who are in Re-stau, on the night when Anubis lay with his arms and his hands over the things behind Osiris, and it when Horus was made to triumph over his enemies."

PLATE 14

§J. **Vignette:** The gods Horus, Osiris, Isis, and (?)

The great godlike rulers in Re-stau are Horus, Osiris, and Isis. The heart of Osiris rejoiceth, and the heart of Horus is glad; and therefore are the east and the west at peace.

"Hail Thoth, who madest Osiris victorious over his enemies, make thou the Osiris Ani, the scribe and teller of the divine offerings of all the gods, to triumph over his enemies in the presence of the ten companies of great godlike rulers who are with Ra and with Osiris and with every god and goddess in the presence of Neb-er-tcher. He hath destroyed his enemies, and he hath destroyed every evil thing belonging unto him."

Rubric: This chapter being recited, the deceased shall come forth by day, purified after death, and [he shall make all] the forms (or transformations) which his heart shall dictate. Now if this chapter be recited over him, he shall come forth upon earth, he shall escape from every fire; and none of the foul things which appertain unto him shall encompass him for everlasting and for ever and for ever.

PLATE

15

Vignette: A seated statue of Ani, the scribe, upon which the ceremony of opening the mouth"*un re*, is being performed by the *sem* priest, clad in a panther's skin and holding in his right hand the instrument Ur *heka i.e.*, "mighty one of enchantments." In front of the statue are: the sepulchral chest, the instruments Seb-ur, Tun-tet, and Temanu, and the object Pesh-en-kef.

THE CHAPTER OF OPENING THE MOUTH OF OSIRIS, THE SCRIBE ANI. To be said: "May Ptah open my mouth, and may the god of my town loose the swathings, even the swathings which are over my mouth . Moreover, may Thoth, being filled and furnished with charms, come and loose the bandages, the bandages of Set which fetter my mouth ; and may the god Tmu hurl them' at those who would fetter [me] with them, and drive them back. May my mouth be opened, may my mouth be unclosed by Shu with his iron knife, wherewith he opened the mouth of the gods. I am Sekhet, and I sit upon the great western side of heaven. I am

PLATE 15

the great goddess Sah among the souls of Annu. Now as concerning every charm and all the words which may be spoken against me, may the gods resist them, and may each and every one of the company of the gods withstand it them."

THE CHAPTER OF BRINGING CHARMS UNTO OSIRIS ANI [IN NETER-KHERT]. [He saith]: "I am Tmu-Khepera, who gave birth unto himself upon the thigh of his divine mother. Those who are in Nu are made wolves, and those who are among the godlike rulers are become hyenas. Behold, I gather together the charm from every place where it is and from every man with whom it is,' swifter than greyhounds and fleeter than light. Hail thou who towest along the *makhent* boat of Ra, the stays of thy sails and of thy rudder are taut in the wind as thou sailest over the Lake of Fire in Neter-khert. Behold, thou gatherest together the charm from every place where it is and from every man with whom it is, swifter than greyhounds and fleeter than light, [the charm] which createth the forms of existence from the mother's thigh (?) and createth the gods from (or in) silence, and which giveth the heat of life unto the gods. Behold, the charm is given unto me from wheresoever it is [and from him with whom it is], swifter than greyhounds and fleeter than light," or, (as others say), "fleeter than a shadow."

Appendix: The following chapter, which generally appears in other early copies of the Book of the Dead, is closely connected with the preceding chapter. It is here taken from the Papyrus of Nebseni.

THE CHAPTER OF CAUSING THE DECEASED TO REMEMBER HIS NAME IN NETER-KHERT. [He saith]: "May my name be given unto me in the great Double House, and may I remember my name in the House of Fire on the night of counting the years and of telling the number of the months. I am with the

Holy One, and I sit on the eastern side of heaven. If any god advanceth unto me, forthwith I proclaim his name."

Vignette: The scribe Ani, clothed in white, and with his heart in his right hand, addressing the god Anubis. Between them is a necklace of several rows of coloured beads, the clasp of which is in the shape of a pylon or gateway, and to which is attached a pectoral bearing a representation of the boat of the sun, wherein is set a scarab, emblematic of the Sun.

CHAPTER XXVII: CHAPTER OF GIVING A HEART UNTO OSIRIS ANI IN THE UNDERWORLD. [Ani saith]: "May my heart be with me in the House of Hearts. May my heart be with me, and may it rest in [me], or I shall not eat of the cakes of Osiris on the eastern side of the Lake of Flowers, [neither shall I have] a boat wherein to go down the Nile, and another wherein to go up, nor shall I go forward in the boat with thee. May my mouth be given unto me that I may speak with it, and my two feet to it walk withal, and my two hands and arms to overthrow my foe. May the doors of heaven be opened unto me; may Seb, the Prince of the gods, open wide his two jaws unto me; may he open my two eyes which are blinded; may he cause me to stretch out my feet which are bound together; and may Anubis make my legs firm that I may stand upon them. May the goddess Sekhet make me to rise so that I may ascend unto heaven, and there may that be done which I command in the House of the *Ka* of Ptah. I know my heart, I have gotten the mastery over my heart, I have gotten the mastery over my two hands and arms, I have gotten the mastery over my feet, and I have gained the power to do whatsoever my ka pleaseth. My soul shall not be shut off from my body at the gates of the underworld; but I shall enter in peace, and I shall come forth in peace."

PLATE 15

THE CHAPTER OF NOT LETTING THE HEART OF OSIRIS, THE SCRIBE OF THE SACRED OFFERINGS OF ALL THE GODS, ANI, TRIUMPHANT, BE DRIVEN FROM HIM IN THE UNDERWORLD. Ani saith: "My heart, my mother; my heart, my mother . My heart whereby I come into being. May there be nothing to withstand me at [my] judgment; may there be no, resistance against me by the Tchatcha; may there be no parting of thee from me in the presence of him who keepeth the Scales! Thou art my *ka* within my body, [which] knitteth and strengtheneth my limbs. Mayest thou come forth in the place of happiness [to which] I advance. May the *Shenit*, who make men to stand fast, not cause my name to stink."

Vignette: Ani holding his soul in the form of a human-headed bird.

CHAPTER OF NOT LETTING THE SOUL OF A MAN BE TAKEN AWAY FROM HIM IN THE UNDERWORLD. Osiris the scribe Ani saith: "I, even I, am he who came forth from the waterflood which I make to overflow and which becometh mighty as the River [Nile]."

Appendix: In many early papyri the text of Chapter LXI. forms part of a longer composition which M. Naville calls Chapters LXI., LX., and LXII., and which reads:—

CHAPTER OF DRINKING WATER IN THE UNDERWORLD. [He saith]: "I, even I, am he who cometh forth from Seb. The flood hath been given unto him, and he hath gotten power over it as Hapi. I, even I, open the two doors of heaven: and the two doors of the watery abyss have been opened unto me by Thoth and by Hapi, the divine twin sons of heaven, who are mighty in splendours. O grant ye that I may gain power over the water, even as Set overcame his foes on the day(?) when he terrified the world.

I have passed by the great ones shoulder against shoulder, even as they have passed by that great and splendid god who is provided [with all things] and whose name is unknown. I have passed by the mighty one of the shoulder. The flood of Osiris hath been passed through by me, and Thoth-Hapi-Tmu, the lord of the horizon, hath opened unto me the flood in his name, 'Thoth, the cleaver of the earth.' I have gained power over the water, even as Set gained power over his foes. I have sailed over heaven. I am Ra. I am the Lion-god. I am the young bull. I have devoured the Thigh, I have seized the flesh. I have gone round about the streams in Seket-Aru. Boundless eternity hath been granted unto me, and, behold, I am the heir of eternity; to me hath been given everlastingness."

Closely connected with the above chapter are the two following short chapters:—

Vignette: The deceased drinking water from a running stream.

THE CHAPTER OF DRINKING WATER AND OF NOT BEING BURNED IN THE FIRE. [The deceased] saith: "Hail, Bull of Amenta. I am brought unto thee, I am the oar of Ra wherewith he ferried over the aged ones; let me not be buried nor consumed. I am Beb, the first-born son of Osiris, who doth wash every god within his eye in Annu. I am the Heir, the exalted the mighty one, the Still [of Heart]. I have made my name to flourish, and I have delivered [it], that I may make myself to live [in remembrance] on this day."

Vignette: The deceased standing near flames of fire.

THE CHAPTER OF NOT BEING SCALDED WITH WATER. [He saith]: "I am the oar made ready for rowing, wherewith Ra ferried over the Aged godlike ones. I carry the moistures of Osiris to the lake away from the flame which cannot be passed ; he is turned aside from the path thereof and he is not burned in the

PLATE 15

fire. I lie down with the *hamemu*; I come unto the Lion's lair, killing and binding; and I follow the path by which he came forth."

Vignette: Ani carrying a sail, emblematic of breath and air.

CHAPTER OF GIVING BREATH IN THE UNDERWORLD. Saith Osiris Ani: "I am the Egg of the Great Cackler, and I watch and guard that great place which the god Seb hath proclaimed upon earth. I live; and it liveth; I grow strong, I live, I sniff the air. I am Utcha-aab, and I go round behind [to protect] his egg. I have thwarted the chance of Set, the mighty one of strength. Hail thou who makest pleasant the world with *tchefa* food, and who dwellest in the blue [sky]; watch over the babe in his cot when he cometh forth unto thee."

Appendix: The two following chapters, which are closely connected with the preceding chapter, are respectively supplied from Naville, *Todtenbuch*, and the Nebseni Papyrus.

Vignette: Anubis leading the deceased into the presence of Osiris.

ANOTHER CHAPTER OF GIVING BREATH. [He saith]: "I am Sabsabu. I am Shu. I draw in the air in the presence of the god of sunbeams as far as the uttermost ends of heaven, as far as the ends of the earth, as far as the bounds of Shu ; and I give breath unto those who become young [again]. I open my mouth, and I see with mine eyes."

Vignette: A man holding a sail in his left hand.

CHAPTER OF SNIFFING THE AIR UPON EARTH. [He saith]: "Hail, Tmu, grant thou unto me the sweet breath which is in thy two nostrils. I embrace the mighty throne which is in Unnu, and I watch and guard the Egg of the Great Cackler. I grow, and it groweth; it groweth, and I grow; I live, and it liveth; I sniff the air, and it sniffeth the air."

Vignette: Ani standing, with a staff in his left hand.

THE CHAPTER OF NOT LETTING THE HEART OF A MAN BE TAKEN AWAY FROM HIM IN THE UNDERWORLD. Saith Osiris Ani, triumphant: "Turn thou back, O messenger of all the gods. Is it that thou art come to carry away this my heart which liveth My heart which liveth shall not be given unto thee. [As I] advance, the gods give ear unto my supplications, and they fall down upon their faces wheresoever they be."

PLATE

16

Vignette: Ani standing, with both hands raised in prayer, before four gods who are seated on a pedestal in the form of Maat; before him is his heart set upon a pedestal.

THE CHAPTER OF NOT LETTING THE HEART OF A MAN BE TAKEN AWAY FROM HIM IN THE UNDERWORLD. Saith Osiris Ani: "Hail, ye who carry away hearts, [hail] ye who steal hearts! ye have done. Homage to you, O ye lords of eternity, ye possessors of everlastingness, "take ye not away this heart of Osiris Ani in your grasp, this heart of Osiris. And cause ye not evil words to spring up against it; because this heart of Osiris Ani is the heart of the one of many names, the mighty one whose words are his limbs, and who sendeth forth his heart to dwell in his body. Heart of Osiris Ani is pleasant unto the gods; he is victorious, he hath gotten power over it; he hath not revealed what hath been done unto it. He gotten power over his own limbs. His heart obeyeth him, he is the lord thereof, it is in his body, and it shall never fall away therefrom. I, Osiris, the scribe Ani, victorious in peace, and triumphant in the beautiful Amenta and on the mountain of eternity, bid thee be obedient unto me in the underworld."

Appendix: The three following chapters, which do not occur in the Ani papyrus, form part of the group of the chapters relating to the heart. They are here supplied from Naville, *Todtenbuch*, Bd. I., Pl. xl., xlii., xxxix.

THE CHAPTER OF THE HEART NOT BEING CARRIED AWAY IN THE UNDERWORLD. He saith: "My heart is with me, and it shall never come to pass that it shall be carried away. I am the lord of hearts, the slayer of the heart. I live in right and in truth, and I have my being therein. I am Horus, a pure heart within a pure body. I live by my word, and my heart doth live. Let not my heart be taken away , let it not be wounded, and may no wounds or gashes be dealt upon me because it hath been taken away from me. May I exist in the body of my father Seb, and in the body of my mother Nut. I have not done evil against the gods; I have not sinned with boasting."

Vignette: The deceased adoring a heart.

THE CHAPTER OF NOT LETTING THE HEART OF A MAN BE DRIVEN AWAY FROM HIM IN THE UNDERWORLD. [He saith]: "My heart, my mother; my heart, my mother. My heart of my life upon earth. May naught rise up against me in judgment in the presence of the lord of the trial; let it not be said concerning me and of that which I have done. 'He hath done deeds against that which is right and true'; may naught be against me in the presence of the great god, the lord of Amenta. Homage to thee, O my heart! Homage to thee, O my heart! Homage to you, O my reins! Homage to you, O ye gods who rule over the divine clouds, and who are

PLATE 16

exalted by reason of your sceptres; speak ye comfortably unto Ra, and make me to prosper before Nehebka." And behold him, even though he be joined to the earth in the innermost parts thereof, and though he be laid upon it, he is not dead in Amenta, but is a glorified being therein.

Vignette: The deceased holding his heart to his breast with his left hand, and kneeling before a monster with a knife in its hand.

[THE CHAPTER OF] NOT LETTING THE HEART OF THE DECEASED BE CARRIED AWAY IN THE UNDERWORLD. [Saith he]: "Hail, Lion-god! I am Un. That which I hate is the block of the god. Let not this my heart be taken away from me by the Fighter in Annu. Hail thou who dost bind Osiris, and who hast seen Set! Hail thou who returnest after smiting and destroying him. This heart sitteth and weepeth in the presence of Osiris; it hath with it the staff for which it entreated him. May there be given unto me for it, may there be decreed unto me for it the hidden things of the heart in the house of Usekh-hra; may there be granted unto it food at the bidding of the Eight. Let not this my heart be" taken from me! I make thee to dwell in thy place, joining together hearts in Sekhet-hetepu, and years of strength in all places of strength, carrying away food (?) at thy it moment with thy hand according to thy great strength. My heart is placed upon the altars of Tmu , who leadeth it to the den of Set; he hath given unto me my heart, whose will hath been done by the godlike rulers in Neter-khert. When they find the leg and the swathings they bury them."

Vignette: Ani and his wife Thuthu, each holding the emblem of air in the left hand, and drinking water with the right from a pool, on the borders of which are palm trees laden with fruit.

THE CHAPTER OF BREATHING THE AIR AND OF HAVING POWER OVER THE WATER IN THE UNDERWORLD. Saith Osiris

Ani: "Open to me! Who art thou then, and whither dost thou fare? I am one of you. Who is it with thee? It is Merti. Separate thou from him, each from each, when thou enterest the Mesqen. He letteth me sail to the temple of the divine beings who have found their faces. The name of the boat is 'Assembler of Souls'; the name of the oars is 'Making the hair to stand on end'; the name it of the hold is 'Good'; and the name of the rudder is 'Making straight for the middle' . . . Grant ye to me vessels of milk together with cakes, loaves of bread, cups of drink, and flesh in the temple of Anubis."

Rubric: If this chapter be known [by Ani] he shall go in after having come forth from the underworld.

Vignette: Ani kneeling beside a pool of water, where grows a sycamore tree; in the tree appears the goddess Nut pouring water into Ani's hands from a vessel

THE CHAPTER OF SNIFFING THE AIR, AND OF GETTING POWER OVER THE WATERS IN THE UNDERWORLD. Saith Osiris Ani: "Hail, sycamore tree of the goddess Nut! Grant thou to me of the water and the air which are in thee. I embrace thy throne which is in Unnu and I watch and guard the egg of the Great Cackler. It groweth, I grow; it liveth, I live; it sniffeth the air, I sniff the air, I the Osiris Ani, in triumph."

Vignette: Ani seated upon a chair before a table of offerings; in his right hand he holds the *kherp* sceptre and in his left a staff.

(I) THE CHAPTER OF NOT DYING A SECOND TIME IN THE UNDERWORLD. Saith Osiris Ani: "My place of hiding is opened, my place of hiding is revealed! Light hath shone in the darkness. The eye of Horus hath ordered my coming into being, and the god Apuat hath nursed me. I have hidden myself with you, O ye stars

PLATE 16

that never set. My brow is like unto that of Ra; my face is open; my heart is upon its throne; I utter words, and I know; in very truth, I am Ra himself. I am not treated with scorn, and violence is not done unto me. Thy father, the son of Nut, liveth for thee. I am thy first-born, and I see thy mysteries. I am crowned like unto the king of the gods, and I shall not die a second time in the underworld."

Vignette: The mummy of Ani embraced by Anubis, the god of the dead.

THE CHAPTER OF NOT CORRUPTING IN THE UNDERWORLD.

Saith Osiris Ani: "O thou who art without motion like unto Osiris! O thou who art without motion like unto Osiris! O thou whose limbs are without motion like unto [those of] Osiris! Let not thy limbs be without motion, let them not corrupt, let them not pass away, let them not decay; let it be done unto me even as if I were the god Osiris."

Rubric: If this chapter be known by the Osiris Ani, he shall not corrupt in the underworld.

Vignette: A doorway. By one post stands the soul of Ani in the form of a human-headed hawk and by the other the bird.

THE CHAPTER OF NOT PERISHING AND OF BECOMING ALIVE IN THE UNDERWORLD. Saith Osiris Ani: "Hail, children of:' Shu! Hail, children of Shu, [children of] the place of the dawn, who as the children of light have gained possession of his crown. May I rise up and may I fare forth like Osiris."

Vignette: Ani the scribe standing with his back to a block and knife

THE CHAPTER OF NOT ENTERING IN UNTO THE BLOCK. Saith Osiris Ani: "The four bones of my neck and of my back are joined together for me in heaven by Ra, the guardian of the earth. This was granted on the day when my rising up out of weakness upon my two feet was ordered, on the day when the hair was cut off. The bones of my neck and of my back have been joined together by Set and by the company of the gods, even as they were in the time that is past; may nothing happen to break them apart. Make ye [me] strong against my father's murderer. I have gotten power over the two earths. Nut hath joined together my bones, and [I] behold [them] as they were in the time that is past [and I] see [them] even in the same order as they were [when] the gods had not come into being in visible forms. I am Penti, I, Osiris the scribe Ani, triumphant, am the heir of the great gods."

Text [CHAPTER XCIIIA.]: ANOTHER CHAPTER. [Saith Osiris Ani]: "So then shall no evil things be done unto me by the fiends, neither shall I be gored by the horns [of Khepera]; and the manhood of Ra, which is the head of Osiris, shall not be swallowed up. Behold me, I enter into my homestead, and I reap the harvest. The gods speak with me. Gore thou not them, O Ra-khepera. In very truth sickness shall not arise in the eye of Tmu nor shall it be destroyed. Let me be brought to an end, may I not be carried into the East to take part in the festivals of the fiends who are my enemies ; may no cruel gashes be made in me. I, Osiris, the scribe Ani, the teller of the divine offerings of all the gods, triumphant with happy victory, the lord to be revered. am not carried away into the East."

THE CHAPTER OF NOT LETTING THE HEAD OF A MAN BE CUT OFF FROM HIM IN THE UNDERWORLD. Saith Osiris Ani: "I am the great One, son of the great One; I am Fire, the son of Fire, to whom was given his head after it had been cut off. The head of Osiris was not carried away from him; let not the head of Osiris Ani be carried away from him. I have knit together my bones, I have made myself whole and sound; I have become young once more; I am Osiris, the Lord of eternity."

Vignette: The mummy of Ani lying on a bier; above is his soul in the form of a human-headed bird, holding *shen*, the emblem of eternity, in its claws. At the head and foot stands an incense burner with fire in it.

THE CHAPTER OF CAUSING THE SOUL TO BE UNITED TO ITS BODY IN THE UNDERWORLD. Saith Osiris Ani: "Hail, thou god Annitu! Hail, O Runner, dwelling in thy hall! O thou great god, grant thou" that my soul may come unto me from wheresoever it may be. If it would tarry, then bring thou unto me my soul from wheresoever it may be. [If] thou findest [me], O Eye of Horus,

PLATE 17

make thou me to stand up like those beings who are like unto Osiris and who never lie down in death. Let not Osiris Ani, triumphant, triumphant, lie down in death in Annu, the land wherein souls are joined unto their bodies, even in thousands. My soul doth bear away with it my victorious spirit whithersoever it goeth If it would tarry, grant thou that my soul may look upon my body. [If] thou findest [me], O Eye of Horus, make thou me to stand up like unto those Hail, ye gods, who row in the boat of the lord of millions of years, who tow it above the underworld, who make it to pass over the ways of Nu, who make souls to enter into their glorified bodies, whose hands are filled with righteousness, and whose fingers grasp your sceptres, destroy ye the foe. The boat of the Sun rejoiceth, and the great god advanceth in peace. Behold [ye gods], grant that this soul of Osiris Ani may come forth triumphant before the gods, and triumphant before you, from the eastern horizon of heaven, to follow unto the place where it was yesterday, in peace, in peace, in Amenta. May he behold his body, may he rest in his glorified frame, may he never perish, and may his body never see corruption."

Rubric: To be said over a golden [figure of a] soul inlaid with precious stones, which is to be placed on the neck of Osiris.

Vignette: Ani's soul, in the form of a human-headed bird, standing in front of a pylon.

THE CHAPTER OF NOT LETTING THE SOUL OF A MAN BE CAPTIVE IN THE UNDERWORLD. Saith Osiris Ani: "Hail thou who art exalted, thou who art adored, thou mighty one of souls, thou Ram (or Soul), possessor of terrible power, who dost put fear of thee into the hearts of the gods, thou who art crowned upon thy mighty throne! It is he who maketh the path for the *khu* and for the soul of Osiris Ani. I am furnished [with that which I need], I am a *khu* furnished [with that which I need], I have made my way unto the place wherein are Ra and Hathor."

Rubric: If this chapter be known, Ani shall become like unto a shining being fully equipped in the underworld. He shall not be stopped at any door in the underworld from going in and coming out millions of times.

Vignette: Ani standing at the doorway of the tomb; and Ani's shadow, accompanied by his soul.

THE CHAPTER OF OPENING THE TOMB TO THE SOUL OF THE SHADOW, OF COMING FORTH BY DAY, AND OF GETTING POWER OVER THE LEGS. Saith Osiris, the scribe Ani, triumphant: "The place of bondage is opened, that which was shut is opened, and; the place of bondage is opened unto my soul [according to the bidding of] the eye of Horus. I have bound and stablished glories upon the brow of Ra. [My] steps are made long, [my] thighs are lifted up; I have passed along the great path, and my limbs are strong. 1 am Horus, the avenger of his father, and I bring the *ureret* crown to rest upon its place. The path of souls is opened [to my soul]."

PLATE

18

My soul seeth the great god within the boat of Ra on the day of souls. My soul is in the front among those who tell the years. Come; the eye of Horus, which stablisheth glories upon the brow of Ra and rays of light upon the faces of those who are with the limbs of Osiris, hath delivered my soul. O shut ye not in my soul, fetter ye not my shade may it behold the great god within the shrine on the day of the judgment of souls, may it repeat the words of Osiris. May those beings whose dwelling-places are hidden, who fetter the limbs of Osiris, who fetter the souls of the khu, who shut in the shade[s] of the dead and can do evil unto me-may they do no evil unto me, may they turn away their path from me. Thy heart is with thee; may my soul and my khu be prepared against their attack. May I sit down among the great rulers who dwell in their abodes; may my soul not be set in bondage by those who fetter the limbs of Osiris, and who fetter souls, and who shut in the shade[s] of the dead. The place which thou possessest, is it not Heaven?"

Rubric: If this chapter be known, he shall come forth by day and his soul shall not be shut in.

Vignette: Ani kneeling, with both hands raised in adoration, by the side of the Seker boat placed upon its sledge.

THE CHAPTER OF WALKING WITH THE TWO LEGS, AND OF COMING FORTH UPON EARTH. Saith Osiris Ani: "Thou hast done all thy work, O Seker, thou hast done all thy work, O Seker, in thy dwelling place within my legs in the underworld. I shine above the Leg of the Sky, I come forth from heaven; I recline with the glorified spirits. Alas! I am weak and feeble; alas! I am weak and feeble. I walk. I am weak and feeble in the presence of those who gnash with the teeth in the underworld, I Osiris, the scribe Ani, triumphant in peace."

Vignette: The emblem of Amenta and Ani standing with a staff in his left hand.

THE CHAPTER OF PASSING THROUGH AMENTA, AND OF COMING FORTH BY DAY. Saith Osiris Ani: "The hour openeth; the head of Thoth is sealed up; perfect is the eye of Horus. I have delivered the eye of Horus which shineth with splendours on the forehead of Ra, the father of the gods. I am the same Osiris, dwelling in Amenta. Osiris knoweth his day and that he shall not live therein; nor shall I live therein. I am the Moon among the gods; I shall not come to an end. Stand up, therefore, O Horus; Osiris hath counted thee among the gods."

THE CHAPTER OF COMING FORTH BY DAY, AND OF LIVING AFTER DEATH. Saith Osiris Ani: "Hail, Only One, shining from the Moon! Hail, Only One, shining from the Moon! Grant that this Osiris Ani may come forth among the multitudes which

PLATE 18

are round about thee; let him be established as a dweller among the shining ones; and let the underworld be opened unto him. And behold Osiris, Osiris Ani shall come forth by day to do his will upon earth among the living."

Vignette: Ani, standing with both hands raised in adoration before a ram crowned with plumes and disk; in front of the ram is a table, upon which are a libation vase and a lotus flower.

THE CHAPTER OF COMING FORTH BY DAY, HAVING PASSED THROUGH THE TOMB. Saith Osiris Ani: "Hail Soul, thou mighty one of strength! Verily I am here, I have come, I behold thee. I have passed through the underworld, I have seen [my] father Osiris, I have scattered the gloom of night. I am his beloved one. I have come; I behold my father Osiris. I have stabbed Set to the heart. I have done the things [needed] by my father Osiris. I have opened every way in heaven and upon earth. I am the son beloved of his father Osiris . I have become a ruler, I have become glorious, I am furnished [with what I need]. Hail, all ye gods, and all ye shining ones, make ye a way for me, the Osiris, the scribe Ani, triumphant."

Vignette: Ani, with a staff in his left hand, standing before a door.

THE CHAPTER OF MAKING A MAN TO RETURN TO SEE AGAIN HIS HOME UPON EARTH. Saith Osiris Ani: "I am the Lion-god coming forth with strides. I have shot forth arrows, I have wounded [the prey], I have wounded the prey. I am the Eye of Horus; I have opened the eye of Horus in his hour. I am come unto the furrows. Let Osiris Ani come in peace."

Vignette: Ani piercing a serpent.

ANOTHER CHAPTER OF ONE WHO COMETH FORTH BY DAY AGAINST HIS FOES IN THE UNDERWORLD. Saith Osiris

Ani: "I have divided the heavens, I have passed through the horizon, I have traversed the earth, [following] upon his footsteps. I am borne away by the mighty and shining ones because, behold, I am furnished with millions of years which have magic virtues. I eat with my mouth, I chew with my jaws; and, behold, I am the god who is the lord of the underworld: May there be given unto me, Osiris Ani, that which abideth for ever without corruption."

PLATE

19

Vignette: Ani standing, with both hands raised in adoration, before Ra, hawk-headed and seated in a boat floating upon the sky. On the bows sits Heru-pa-khrat (Harpocrates) or, "Horus the child"; and the side is ornamented with feathers of Maat, and the *utchat*. The handles of the oars and the tops of the rowlocks are shaped as hawks' heads, and on the blades of the oars are two utchat.

A HYMN OF PRAISE TO RA WHEN HE RISETH UPON THE HORIZON, AND WHEN HE SETTETH IN THE [LAND OF] LIFE. Saith Osiris, the scribe Ani: "Homage to thee, O Ra, when thou risest [as] Tmu-Heru-khuti (Harmachis), Thou art adored [by me] when thy beauties are before mine eyes, and when thy shining rays [fall] upon my body. Thou goest forth in peace in the *Sektet* boat with [fair] winds, and thy heart is glad; [thou goest forth] in the *Atet* boat, and its heart is glad. Thou stridest over the heavens in peace, and thy foes are cast down; the never-resting stars sing hymns of praise unto thee, and the stars which never set glorify thee as thou sinkest in the horizon of Manu, O thou who art beautiful in the two parts of heaven, thou lord who livest and art established, O my lord! Homage to thee, O thou who art Ra when thou risest, and Tmu when thou settest in beauty. Thou risest and shinest upon the back of thy mother [the sky], O thou who art crowned king of the gods. Nut doth homage unto thee, and everlasting and never-changing order embraceth thee at morn and at eve. Thou stridest over the heaven, being glad of heart, and the Lake Testes is at peace. The Fiend hath fallen to the ground; his arms and his hands have been hewn off, and the knife hath severed the joints of his body. Ra hath a fair wind ; the *Sektet* boat goeth forth and sailing along it cometh into port. The gods of the south and of the north, of the west and of the east praise thee, from whom all forms of life came into being. Thou sendest forth the word, and the earth is flooded with silence, O thou only One, who livedst in heaven before ever the earth and the mountains were made. O Runner, Lord, only One, thou maker of things which are, thou hast moulded the tongue of the company of the gods, thou hast drawn forth whatsoever cometh from the waters, and thou springest up from them over the flooded land of the Lake of Horus . Make me to sniff the air which cometh forth from thy nostrils, and the north wind which cometh forth from thy mother [the Sky]. Make thou glorious my shining form, O Osiris, make thou strong my soul. Thou art worshipped in peace, O lord of the gods, thou art exalted by reason of thy wondrous works. Shine with thy rays of light upon my body day by day, upon me, Osiris, the scribe, the teller of the divine offerings it of all the gods, the overseer of the granary of the lords of Abydos, the royal it scribe in truth, who loveth him (*i.e.*, Ra); Ani, triumphant in peace."

PLATE 19

Vignette: Ani, standing with both hands raised in adoration. Behind him is his wife:

Ausar nebt per qematet en Amen Thuthu.

Osiris, the lady of the house, priestess of Amen, Thuthu.

A HYMN OF PRAISE. "O OSIRIS, lord of eternity, Un-nefer, Horus of the two horizons, whose forms are manifold, whose creations are without number, Ptah-Seker-Tem in Annu, the lord of the tomb, and the creator of Memphis and of the gods, the guide of the underworld, whom [the gods] glorify when thou settest in Nut. Isis embraceth thee in peace, and she driveth away the fiends from the mouth of thy paths. Thou turnest thy face upon Amenta, thou makest the world to shine as with smu metal. The dead rise up to behold thee, they breathe the air and they look upon thy face when the disk shineth on its horizon; their hearts are at peace for that they behold thee, O thou who art eternity and everlastingness."

[Litany]: "Homage to thee, [O lord of] starry deities in An, and of heavenly beings in Kher-aba; thou god Unti, who art more glorious than the gods who are hidden in Annu.

"Homage to thee, O An in Antes (?), Horus, thou dweller in both horizons, with long strides thou stridest over heaven, O thou who dwellest in both horizons.

"Homage to thee, O soul of everlastingness, thou Soul who dwellest in Tattu, Un-nefer, son of Nut; thou art lord of Akert.

"Homage to thee in thy dominion over Tattu; the urerit crown is established upon thy head; thou art the One whose strength is in himself, and thou dwellest in peace in Tattu.

"Homage to thee, O lord of the acacia tree, the Seker boat is set upon its sledge; thou turnest back the Fiend, the worker of evil, and thou causest the *utchat* to rest upon its seat.

"Homage to thee, O thou who art mighty in thine hour, thou great and mighty god, dweller in An-rut-f, lord of eternity and creator of everlastingness; thou art the lord of Suten-henen.

"Homage to thee, O thou who restest upon Right and Truth, thou art the lord of Abtu, and thy limbs are joined unto Ta-sertet; thou art he to whom fraud and guile are hateful.

"Homage to thee, O thou who art within thy boat, thou bringest Hapi (*i.e.*, the Nile) forth from his source; the light shineth upon thy body, and thou art the dweller in Nekhen.

"Homage to thee, O creator of the gods, thou King of the North and of the South; O Osiris, victorious, ruler of the world in thy gracious seasons; thou art the lord of the world.

"O grant thou unto me a path whereon I may pass in peace, for I am just and true; I have not spoken lies wittingly, nor have I done aught with deceit."

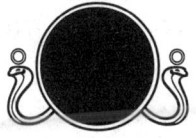

PLATE

20

ignette: Osiris and Isis in a sepulchral shrine.
A HYMN OF PRAISE To RA WHEN HE RISETH IN THE EASTERN PART OF THE HEAVEN. They who are in his train rejoice, and lo! Osiris Ani in triumph saith "Hail, thou Disk, thou lord of rays, who risest in the horizon day by day. Shine thou with thy beams of light upon the face of Osiris Ani, who is victorious: for he singeth hymns of praise unto thee at dawn, and he maketh thee to set at eventide with words of adoration. May the soul of Osiris Ani, the triumphant one, come forth with thee from heaven, may he go forth in the *matet* boat, may he come into port in the *sektet* boat, may he cleave his path among the never resting stars in the heavens."

Osiris Ani, being at peace and in triumph, adoreth his lord, the lord of eternity, saying: "Homage to thee, O Horus of the two horizons, who art Khepera the self-created; when thou risest on the horizon and sheddest thy beams of light upon the lands of the North and the South thou art beautiful, yea beautiful, and all the gods rejoice when they behold thee, the King of heaven. The goddess Nebt-Unnet is stablished upon thy head; her portions of the south and of the north are upon thy brow ; she taketh her place before thee. The god Thoth is stablished in the bows of thy boat to destroy utterly all thy foes. Those who dwell in the underworld come forth to meet thee, bowing in homage as they come towards thee, and to behold [thy] beautiful Image. And I have come before thee that I may be with thee to behold thy Disk every day. May I not be shut in the tomb, may I not be turned back , may the limbs of my body be made new again when I view thy beauties, even as do all thy favoured ones, because I am one of those who worshipped thee whilst they lived upon earth. May I come in unto the land of eternity, may I come even unto the everlasting land, for behold, O my lord, this hast thou ordained for me."

And lo, Osiris Ani, triumphant in peace, the triumphant one, saith Homage to thee, O thou who risest in thy horizon as Ra, thou art stablished by a law which changeth not nor can it be altered. Thou passest over the sky, and every face watcheth thee and thy course, for thou hast been hidden from their gaze. Thou dost show thyself at dawn and at eventide day by day. The *Sektet* boat, wherein is thy majesty, goeth forth with might; thy beams shine upon [all] faces; [the number] of thy yellow rays cannot be known, nor can thy bright beams be told. The lands of the gods, and the colours of the eastern lands of Punt, must be seen, ere that which is hidden [in thee] may be measured [by man]. Alone and by thyself thou dost manifest thyself [when] thou comest into being above Nu. May Ani advance, even as thou dost advance; may he never cease [to go forward], even as thy majesty ceaseth not [to go forward], even though it be for a moment; for with strides dost thou in one little moment pass over the spaces which would need hundreds of thousands and millions of years [for man to pass over; this]

PLATE 20

thou doest, and then dost thou sink down. Thou puttest an end to the hours of the night, and thou dost number them, even thou; thou endest them in thine own appointed season, and the earth becometh light. Thou settest thyself before thy handiwork in the likeness of Ra; thou risest in the horizon."

Osiris, the scribe Ani, triumphant, declareth his praise of thee when thou shinest, and when thou risest at dawn he crieth in his joy at thy birth:" Thou art crowned with the majesty of thy beauties; thou mouldest thy limbs as thou dost advance, and thou bringest them forth without birth-pangs in the form of Ra , as thou dost climb up into the upper air. Grant thou that I may come unto the heaven which is everlasting, and unto the mountain [where dwell] thy favoured ones. May I be joined unto those shining beings, holy and perfect, who are in the underworld; and may I come forth with them to behold thy beauties when thou shinest at eventide and goest to thy mother Nut".

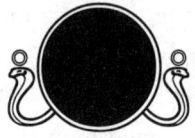

PLATE

21

"Thou dost place thy disk in the west, and my two hands are [raised] in adoration [of thee] when thou settest as a living being. Behold, thou art the maker of eternity, and thou art adored [when] thou settest in the heavens. I have given my heart unto thee without wavering, O thou who art mightier than the gods."

Osiris Ani, triumphant, saith: "A hymn of praise to thee, O thou who risest like unto gold, and who dost flood the world with light on the day of thy birth. Thy mother giveth thee birth upon [her] hand, and thou dost give light unto the course of the Disk. O thou mighty Light, who shinest in the heavens, thou dost strengthen the generations of men with the Nile-flood, and dost cause gladness in all lands, and in all cities, and in all the temples. Thou art glorious by reason of thy splendours, and thou makest strong thy *ka* with *hu* and *tchefau* foods. O thou who art the mighty one of victories, thou who art the Power of [all] Powers, who dost make strong thy throne against the

PLATE 21

powers of wickedness, who art glorious in majesty in the *sektet* boat, and who art exceeding (1-6) mighty in the *atet* boat, make thou glorious Osiris Ani with victory in the netherworld; grant thou that in the underworld he may be void of sin. I pray thee to put away [his] faults behind thee; grant that he may be one of thy venerable servants who are with the shining ones; may he be joined unto the souls which are in Ta-sertet; and may he journey into the Sekhet-Aaru by a prosperous and happy path, he the Osiris, the scribe Ani, triumphant. "Thou shalt come forth into heaven, thou shalt pass over the sky, thou shalt be joined unto the starry deities. Praises shall be offered unto thee in thy boat, thou shalt be hymned in the diet boat, thou shalt behold Ra within his shrine, thou shalt set together with his disk day by day, thou shalt see the ant fish when it springeth into being in the waters of turquoise, and thou shalt see the *abtu* fish in his hour. May it come to pass that the Evil One shall fall when he layeth a snare to destroy me, and may the joints of his neck and of his back be cut in sunder." "Ra [saileth] with a fair wind, and the sektet boat draweth on and cometh into port. The mariners of Ra rejoice, and the heart of Nebt-ankh is glad, for the enemy of her lord hath fallen to the ground. Thou shalt behold Horus on the watch [in the Boat], and Thoth and Maat upon either side of him. All the gods rejoice when they behold Ra coming in peace to make the hearts of the shining ones to live. May Osiris Ani, triumphant, the scribe of the divine offerings of the lords of Thebes, be with them."

Vignette: Ra, hawk-headed, with the disk upon his head and the emblem of life upon his knees, seated in the solar bark; before him stands Ani with both hands raised in adoration.

TO BE SAID ON THE DAY OF THE MONTH. Osiris Ani, the scribe, triumphant in peace, triumphant, saith: "Ra riseth in his horizon, and the company of his gods follow after the god when he appeareth from his secret place, when he showeth strength and bringeth himself forth from the eastern horizon of heaven at the word of the goddess Nut. They rejoice at the journeyings of Ra, the Ancient One; the Great One rolleth along in his course. Thy joints are knitted together, O Ra, within thy shrine. Thou breathest the winds, thou drawest in the breezes, thou makest thy jaw-bones to eat in thy dwelling on the day when thou dost scent right and truth. Thou turnest aside the godlike followers [who] sail after the sacred boat, in order that they may return again unto the mighty ones according to thy word. Thou numberest thy bones, thou gatherest together thy members; thou turnest thy face towards the beautiful Amenta; thou comest thither renewed day by day. Behold, thou Image of gold, who possessest the splendours of the Disk of heaven, thou lord of terror; thou rollest along and art renewed day by day. Hail, there is rejoicing in the heavenly horizon, and shouts of joy are It raised to the ropes which tow thee along. May the gods who dwell in heaven ascribe praises unto Osiris Ani, when they behold him in triumph, as unto Ra. May Osiris, the scribe Ani, be a prince who is known by the ureret crown; and may the meat offerings and the drink offerings of Osiris Ani, triumphant, be apportioned unto him; may he wax exceeding strong in his body; and may he be the chief of those who are in the presence of Ra. May Osiris, the scribe Ani, triumphant, be strong upon earth and in the world under the earth; and O Osiris, scribe Ani, triumphant, mayest thou rise up strengthened like unto Ra day by day. Osiris Am, triumphant, shall not tarry, nor shall he rest without motion in the earth for ever. Clearly, clearly shall he see with his two eyes, and with his two ears shall he hear what is right and true. Osiris, the scribe Ani, triumphant, cometh back, cometh back from Annu; Osiris Ani, triumphant, is as Ra when he rangeth the oars among the followers of Nu.

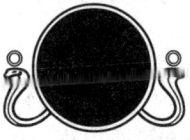

PLATE

22

"Osiris Ani, triumphant, hath not revealed what he hath seen, he hath not, he hath not told again what he hath heard in the house which is hidden. Hail, there are shouts of joy to Osiris Ani, triumphant, for he is a god and the flesh of Ra, he is in the boat of Nu, and his ka is well pleased according to the will of the god. Osiris Ani, triumphant, is in peace, he is triumphant like unto Horus, and he is mighty because he hath divers forms."

Vignette: Ra seated in a boat, sailing across the sky towards the starstudded heaven.

Rubric: These words shall be recited over a boat seven cubits in length, and painted green for the godlike rulers. Then shalt thou make a heaven of stars washed and purified with natron and incense. Behold, thou shalt make an image of Ra upon a table of stone painted yellow, and it shall be placed in the fore-part of the boat. Behold, thou shalt make an image of the dead man whom thou wilt make perfect in strength in the boat; and thou shalt make it to travel in the divine boat of Ra, and Ra himself will look upon it therein. Thou shalt show it to no man but thyself, or to thy father or to thy son; let them watch with their faces, and he shall be seen in the underworld as a messenger of Ra.

Vignette: Ra, hawk-headed, with a disk upon his head, seated in a boat; before him is a large disk.

A HYMN OF PRAISE TO RA ON THE DAY OF THE MONTH WHEREON HE SAILETH IN THE BOAT. [Osiris, the scribe Ani, saith]: "Homage to thee, O thou who art in thy boat! Thou risest, thou risest, thou shinest with thy rays, and thou hast made mankind to rejoice for millions of years according to thy will. Thou showest thy face unto the beings whom thou hast created, O Khepera, in thy boat. Thou hast overthrown Apepi. O ye children of Seb, overthrow ye the foes of Osiris Ani, triumphant, destroy ye the adversaries of righteousness from the boat of Ra. Horus shall cut off your heads in heaven in the likeness of ducks; ye shall fall down upon the earth and become beasts, and into the water in the likeness of fishes. [Osiris, the scribe Ani,] destroyeth every hostile fiend, male and female, whether he passeth through heaven, [or] appeareth upon earth, or cometh forth upon the water, or passeth along before the starry deities; and Thoth strengtheneth them . . . coming forth from Anreti. Osiris, the scribe Ani, is silent, and becometh the second of Ra. Behold thou the god, the great slaughterer, greatly to be feared, he washeth in your blood, he batheth in your gore; Osiris, the scribe Ani, destroyeth them from the boat of his father Ra-Horus. The mother Isis giveth birth unto Osiris, the scribe Ani, triumphant, whose heart liveth, and Nephthys nurseth him ; even as they did for Horus, who drove back the fiends of Sut. They saw the *urertu* crown stablished upon his head, and they fell down upon their

PLATE 22

faces. Behold, O ye shining ones, ye men and gods, ye damned ones, when ye behold Osiris Ani, triumphant like unto Horus and adored by reason of the ureret crown, fall ye down upon your faces; for Osiris Ani is victorious over his foes in the heavens above and [on the earth] beneath, in the presence of the godlike rulers of all the gods and goddesses."

Rubric: These words shall be recited over a great hawk which hath the white crown set upon his head. Then shall the names of Tmu, Shu, Tefnut, Seb, Nut, Osiris, Isis, Nephthys, be written with green colour upon a new table, anointed with unguents and placed in a boat together with a figure of the dead man . Then shall they put incense upon the fire, and set ducks to be roasted . This is a rite of Ra when his boat cometh; and it shall cause the dead man to go with Ra into every place whithersoever he saileth, and the foes of Ra shall be slaughtered in very truth. The Chapter of the *sektet* boat shall be recited on the sixth day of the festival.

The ladder by which the soul passes from the underworld to the body.

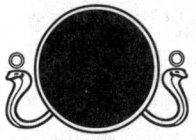

PLATES
23–24

T he whole of Plate 23 and part of Plate 24 contain a repetition of the 18th Chapter of the *Book of the Dead,* which has also been given on Plates 13 and 14. The arrangement of the gods in the vignette is, however, slightly different.

PLATE 24

Vignette: Ani and his wife adoring three gods, who are seated on a pylon or door-shaped pedestal.

THE CHAPTER OF GOING UNTO THE GODLIKE RULERS OF OSIRIS. Osiris, the scribe Ani, triumphant, saith: "My soul hath builded for me a dwelling-place in Tattu. I have waxed strong in the town Pe. I have ploughed [my] fields in all my forms, and my palm tree standeth therein like unto the god Amsu. I eat not that which I abominate, I eat not that which I loathe; that which I abominate I abominate, and I feed not upon filth. There are food offerings and meat for those who shall not be destroyed thereby. I raise not up myself on my two arms unto any abomination, I walk not thereupon with my shoes, because my bread is [made] from white grain, and my ale from the red barley of the Nile. The *sektet* boat and the *atet* boat bring them unto me, and I feed upon them under the trees, whose beautiful branches I myself do know. How glorious do I make the white crown [when] I lift up the uraei! Hail, guardian of the door, who givest peace unto the two lands, bring thou unto me those who make offerings! Grant that I may lift up the earth; that the shining ones may open their arms unto me; that the company of the gods may speak with the words of the shining ones unto Osiris Ani; that the hearts of the gods may direct [him] ; and that they may make him powerful in heaven among the gods who have taken unto themselves visible forms. Yea, let every god and every goddess whom he passeth make Osiris, the scribe Ani, triumphant at the new year. He feedeth upon hearts and consumeth them when he cometh forth from the east. He hath been judged by the forefather of Light. He is a shining one arrayed in heaven among the mighty ones. The food of Osiris, the scribe Ani, triumphant, is even the cakes and ale which are made for their mouths. I go in through the Disk, I come out through the god Ahui. I speak with the followers of the gods, I speak with the Disk, I speak with the shining ones, and the Disk granteth me to be victorious in the blackness of night within Meh-urt near unto his forehead. Behold, I am with Osiris, and I proclaim that which he telleth forth among the mighty ones. He speaketh unto me the words of men, and I listen and 1 tell again unto him the words of the gods. I, Osiris Ani, triumphant, come even as one who is equipped for the journey. Thou raisest up [right and truth] for those who love them. I am a shining one clothed in power, mightier than any other shining one."

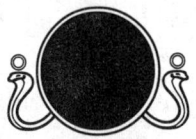

PLATE

25

Vignette: A swallow perched on a conical object painted red and green.

(I) HERE BEGIN THE CHAPTERS OF MAKING TRANSFORMATIONS. THE CHANGING INTO A SWALLOW. Saith Osiris Ani, triumphant: "I am the swallow, [I am] the swallow, [I am] the scorpion, the daughter of Ra. Hail, ye gods, whose scent is sweet; hail, ye gods, whose scent is sweet! Hail, thou Flame, which comest forth from the horizon! Hail, thou who art in the city. May the Guardian of the Bight lead me on. O stretch out up unto me thine bands that I may be able to pass my days in the Island of Flame. I have fared forth with my warrant. I have come with the power thereof. Let the doors be opened unto me . How shall I tell what I have seen therein? Horus was like unto the prince of the sacred bark, and the throne of his father was given unto him. Sut, the son of Nut, also hath gotten the fall which he wrought for Horus. He who is in Sekhem passed judgment upon me. I stretched out my

PLATE 25

hands and my arms unto Osiris. I have passed on to judgment, and I have come that I may speak; grant that I may pass on and deliver my message. I enter in, having been judged; I come out at the door of Neb-er-tcher magnified and glorified. I am found pure at the Great place of passage [of souls]. I have put away my faults. I have done away mine offences. I have cast out the sins which were a part of me. I, even I, am pure, I, even I, am mighty. O ye doorkeepers, I have made my way [unto you]. I am like unto you. I have come forth by day. I have walked with my legs, and I have gotten the power of the footstep wherewith do walk the shining ones of light . I, even I, know the hidden ways to the doors of the Field of Aaru; and , though my body be buried, yet let me rise up; and may I come forth and overthrow all my foes upon earth."

Rubric. If this chapter be known [by the deceased], he shall come forth by day in Neter-khert, and he shall go in again after he hath come forth. if this chapter be not known, he shall not enter in after he hath come forth, nor shall he come forth by day.

Vignette: A golden hawk holding a flail, emblem of rule.

CHAPTER OF CHANGING INTO A GOLDEN HAWK. Saith Osiris Ani: "May I, even I, arise in the *seshet* chamber, like unto a hawk of gold coming forth from his egg. May I fly and may I hover as a hawk, with a back seven cubits wide, and with wings made of emeralds of the South. May I come forth from the *seket* boat , and may my heart be brought unto me from the mountain of the east. May I alight on the *atet* boat, and may those who are in their companies be brought unto me, bowing down as they come. May I rise, may I gather myself together as the beautiful golden hawk [which hath] the head of a *bennu* bird. May I enter into the presence of Ra daily to hear his words, and may I sit down among the mighty gods of Nut. May a homestead be made ready for me, and may offerings of food and drink be put before me therein. May I eat therein; may I become a shining one therein; may I be filled therein to, my heart's fullest desire; may sacred wheat be given unto me to eat. May I, by myself, get power over the guardian of my head."

Vignette: A green hawk, holding a flail, and standing upon a pylon-shaped pedestal.

THE CHAPTER OF CHANGING INTO A SACRED HAWK. Saith Osiris Ani: "Hail, thou mighty one, come unto Tattu. Make thou my paths, and let me pass round [to visit] my thrones. Make me to renew myself and make me to wax strong. Grant that I may be feared, and make me to be a terror. May the gods of the underworld fear me, and may they fight for me in their habitations. Let not him that would do harm unto me draw nigh unto me. Let me walk through the house of darkness. May I , the feeble, clothe and cover myself; and may they (*i.e.*, the gods) not do the like unto me. Hail, ye gods who hear my speech! Hail, ye rulers who are among the followers of Osiris. Be ye therefore silent, O ye gods, [when] the god speaketh with me; he heareth what is right and true. What I speak unto him, do thou also speak, O Osiris. Grant thou that I may go round my course according to the order which cometh forth from thy mouth concerning me. May I see thy forms; may I be able to understand thy will. Grant that I may come forth, that I may get power over my legs, and that I may be like unto Neb-er-tcher upon his throne. May the gods of the underworld fear me, and may they fight for me in their habitations. Grant thou that I may pass on my way with the godlike ones who rise up . May I be set up upon my resting-place like unto the Lord of Life; may I be joined unto Isis, the divine Lady. May the gods make me strong against him that would do harm unto me, and may no one come to see me fall helpless. May

PLATE 25

I pass over the paths , may I come into the furthermost parts of heaven. I entreat for speech with Seb, I make supplication unto Hu and unto Neb-er-tcher that the gods of the underworld may fear me, and that they may fight for me in their habitations, when they see that thou hast provided me with the fowl of the air and the fish of the sea. "I am one of those shining ones who live in rays of light. I have made my form like unto the form [of the god] who cometh out and manifesteth himself in Tattu; for I have become worthy of honour by reason of his honour, and he hath spoken unto thee of the things which concern me. Surely he hath made the fear of me [to go forth], and hath created terror of me! The gods of the . . .

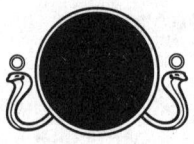

PLATE

26

Underworld fear me, and they fight for me [in their habitations]. I, in very truth I am a shining one and a dweller in light, who hath been created and who hath come into being from the body of the god. I am one of the shining ones who dwell in light, whom Tmu himself hath created, and who have.(come into being from the eyelashes of his eye. He doth create and glorify and make noble the faces of those who live with him. Behold, the only One in Nu! They do homage unto him as he cometh forth from the horizon, and they strike fear of him into the gods and into the shining ones who have come into being with him.

"I am the One among the worms which the eye of the Lord, the only One, hath created. And lo! before Isis was, and when Horus was not yet, I had waxed strong, and flourished. I had grown old, and I had become greater than they who were among the shining ones who had come into being with him, and I, even I, arose in the form of

PLATE 26

a sacred hawk , and Horus made me worthy in the form of his own soul, to take possession of all that belongeth unto Osiris in the underworld. The double Lion-god, the warder of the things that belong to the house of the *nemmes* crown which is in his hiding place, saith unto me: 'Get thee back to the heights of heaven, seeing that through Horus thou hast become glorified in thy form; the *nemmes* crown is not for thee; thou hast speech even unto the ends of heaven.' I, the guardian, take possession of the things which belong to Horus and Osiris in the underworld. Horus telleth aloud unto me that which (28) his father had said concerning me in years [gone by], on the day of the burial [of Osiris]. I have given unto thee the *nemmes* of the double Lion-god which I possess, that thou mayest pass onward and mayest travel over the path of heaven, and that they who dwell on the confines of the horizon may see thee, and that the gods of the underworld may fear thee and may fight for thee in their habitations. The god Auhet is of them. The gods, the lords of the boundaries of heaven, they who are the warders of the shrine of the lord, the only One, have fallen before my words, have fallen down before [my] words. Hail! He that is exalted upon his tomb is on my side, and he hath bound upon my head the *nemmes* crown. The double Lion-god hath decreed it, the god Auhet hath made a way for me. I, even I, am exalted, and the double Lion-god hath bound the *nemmes* crown on me, and my head covering hath been given unto me. He hath stablished my heart through his strength and through his great might, and I shall not fall through Shu. I am Hetep, the lord of the two uraei, the being who is adored. I know the shining god, and his breath is in my body. I shall not be driven back by the Bull which causeth men to tremble, but I shall come daily into the house of the double Lion-god, and I shall come forth therefrom into the house of Isis. I shall behold sacred things which are hidden, there shall be done unto me holy hidden rites,

I shall see what is there; my words shall make full the majesty of Shu, and they shall drive away evil hap. I, even I, am Horus who dwell in splendours. I have gained power over his crown, I have gained power over his radiance , and I have travelled over the remotest parts of heaven. Horus is upon his throne, Horus is upon his seat. My face is like unto that of a divine hawk. I am one who hath been armed by his lord. I have come forth from Tattu. I have seen Osiris, I have risen up on either side of him. Nut [hath shrouded me]. The gods behold me, and I have beheld the gods. The eye of Horus hath consumed me, who dwell in darkness. The gods stretch forth their arms unto me. I rise up, I get the mastery, and I drive back evil which opposeth me. The gods open unto me the holy way, they see my form, and they hear my words which I utter in their presence. O ye gods of the underworld, who set yourselves up against me, and who resist the mighty ones, the stars which never set have led me on my way. I have passed along the holy paths of the *hemtet* chamber unto your lord, the exceedingly mighty and terrible Soul. Horus hath commanded that ye lift up your faces to look upon me. I have risen up in the likeness of a divine hawk, and Horus hath set me apart in the likeness of his own soul, to take possession of that which belongeth unto Osiris in the underworld. I have passed along the way, I have travelled on and I have come even among those who live in their hiding places and who guard the house of Osiris. 1 speak unto them of his power and I make them to know the terrible power of him that is provided with two horns [to fight] against Sut; and they know who hath carried off the sacred food which the power (?) of Tmu had brought for him. The gods of the underworld have proclaimed a happy coming for me. O Ye who live in your hiding places and who guard the house of Osiris, and who have magnified your names, grant ye that I may come unto you. I bind together and I gather up your powers, and I order the strength of

PLATE 26

the paths of those who guard the horizon of the *hemtet* of heaven.
I have stablished their habitations for Osiris, I have ordered his
ways, I have done what hath been bidden. I have come forth from
Tattu, I have beheld Osiris, I have spoken unto him concerning
the things of his son, the divine Prince whom he loveth. There is
a wound in the heart of Set, and I have seen him who is without

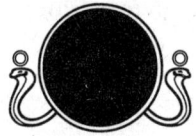

PLATE

27

L ife. O, I have made them to know the plans of the gods which Horus hath devised at the bidding of his father Osiris. Hail, lord, thou most terrible and mighty soul! Let me come, even me, let me lift myself up! I have opened and passed through the underworld. I have opened the paths of the warders of heaven and of the warders of the earth. I have not been driven back by them; and I have lifted up thy face, O lord of eternity."

The following is the end of the 78th chapter according to the Paris papyrus quoted by Naville—

"Thou art exalted upon thy throne, O Osiris. Thou hearest joyful things, O Osiris. Thy, strength is vigorous, O Osiris. Thy head is bound to thy body, O Osiris. Thy brow is made firm, O Osiris. Thy heart is joyful. O be thou pleased to establish gladness for thy servants. Thou art stablished as a bull of Amenta. Thy son Horus is crowned king upon thy throne; all life is with him. Unto thy son are given millions of years, and the fear of him shall endure for untold ages.

PLATE 27

The company of the gods shall fear him. Unto thy son is given of the company of the gods; he changeth not his word. Horus is the food and the altar. I go to unite myself unto [my] father; and deliverance cometh from [my] father, from [my] brother, and from the friend of Horns. Horus is in the following of his father. He dwelleth amid decay. He ruleth Khem. To thy son have the gods given the crown of millions of years, and for millions of years it maketh him to live in the eye [of Horus], the single eye of the god [which is called] Nebt-er-tcher, the queen of the gods."

Vignette: The deceased kneeling, with both hands raised in adoration, before three gods.

THE CHAPTER OF BEING AMONG THE COMPANY OF THE GODS AND OF BEING CHANGED INTO THE PRINCE OF THE GODLIKE RULERS. [The deceased] saith: "Homage to thee, O Tmu, lord of heaven, thou creator of things which are and which come forth from the earth; who makest to come into being that which is sown, the lord of things which shall be, the begetter of the gods, the great god who made himself, the lord of life who maketh mankind to flourish. Homage to you, O ye lords of creation, ye pure being whose abodes are hidden. Homage to you, O ye lords of eternity, whose forms are hidden, and whose dwelling-places are unknown. Homage to you, O ye gods who dwell in the abode (?) of the flooded lands. Homage to you, O ye gods who live in the underworld. Homage to you, O ye gods who dwell in heaven. Grant ye that I may come [unto you], for I know you. I am pure, I am holy, I am mighty, I have a soul, 1 have become powerful, I am glorious; I have brought unto you perfume and incense, and natron. Blot out from your hearts whatsoever ye have in them against me. I have come, having done away all the evil which dwelleth in your hearts against me, I have made an end of all the sin which I committed against you; I have brought unto you that which is good, I have made to come unto you that which is right and true. I, even I, know you, I know your names, I know your forms which are not known, which come into being with you. I have come unto you.

I have risen among men like unto the god, living among the gods. I am strong before you like unto the god who is exalted upon his resting-place; when he cometh the gods rejoice, and goddesses and mortal women are glad when they behold him. I have come unto you. I have risen upon the throne of Ra, I sit upon my seat in the horizon. I receive offerings upon my altar, 1 drink drink-offerings at eventide as one made noble by the lord of mortals. I am exalted even as the holy god, the lord of the great House. The gods rejoice when they see him in his beautiful manifestation on the body of Nut, who giveth birth unto him daily."

Vignette: The serpent Seta, with human legs.

THE CHAPTER OF CHANGING INTO SETA. Osiris Ani, triumphant, saith: "I am the serpent Seta, whose years are many. I lie down and I am born day by day. I am the serpent Seta, which dwelleth in the limits of the earth. I lie down, I am born, I renew myself, I grow young day by day."

Vignette: A crocodile upon a pylon or doorway.

THE CHAPTER OF CHANGING INTO A CROCODILE. Saith Osiris Ani, triumphant: "I am the crocodile which dwelleth in terror, I am the sacred crocodile and I cause destruction. I am the great fish in Kamui. I am the lord to whom homage is paid in Sekhem; and Osiris Ani is the lord to whom homage is paid in Sekhem."

Vignette: The god Ptah in a shrine, before which is a table of offerings.

PLATE 27

THE CHAPTER OF CHANGING INTO PTAH. Saith Osiris Ani, triumphant: "I eat bread, I drink ale, I put on apparel, I fly like a hawk, I cackle like a goose, and I alight upon the path hard by the hill of the dead on the festival of the great Being. That which is abominable, that which is abominable, have I not eaten; and that which is foul have I not swallowed. That which my *ka* doth abominate hath not entered into my body. I have lived according to the knowledge of the glorious gods. I live and I get strength from their bread, I get strength when I eat it beneath the shade of the tree of Hathor, my lady. I make an offering, and I make bread in Tattu, and oblations in Annu. I array myself in the robe of the goddess Matait, and I rise up and I sit me down wheresoever my heart desireth . My head is like unto the head of Ra; when my limbs are gathered together, I am like unto Tmu. The four regions of Ra are the limits of the earth. I come forth; my tongue is like unto the tongue of Ptah, my throat is even as that of Hathor, and I tell forth the words of my father Tmu with my lips. He it is who constrained the handmaid, the wife of Seb; and unto him are bowed [all] heads, and there is fear of him. Hymns of praise are sung in honour of my mighty deeds , and I am accounted the heir of Seb, the lord of the earth, the protector. The god Seb giveth cool water, he maketh his dawnings to be mine. They who dwell in Annu bow down their heads before me, for I am their bull. I grow strong from moment to moment; my loins are made strong for millions of years."

Vignette: A Ram.

THE CHAPTER OF CHANGING INTO THE SOUL OF Tmu. Saith Osiris Ani, triumphant: "I have not entered into the house of destruction; I have not been brought to naught, I have not known decay. I am Ra who come forth from Nu, the divine Soul, the creator of his own limbs. Sin is an abomination unto me, and

I look not thereon; I cry not out against right and truth, but I have my being therein. I am the god Hu, and I never die in my name of 'Soul.' I have brought myself into being together with Nu in my name of 'Khepera.' In their forms have I come into being in the likeness of Ra. I am the lord of light."

Vignette: A *bennu* bird

THE CHAPTER OF CHANGING INTO A *bennu*.

Saith Osiris, the scribe Ani, triumphant in peace: "I came into being from unformed matter, I created myself in the image of the god Khepera, and I grew in the form of plants. I am hidden in the likeness of the Tortoise. I am formed out of the atoms of all the gods. I am the yesterday of the four [quarters of the world], and I am the seven uraei which came into existence in the East, the mighty one who illumineth the nations by his body. He is god in the likeness of Set; and Thoth dwelleth in the midst of them by judgment of the dweller in Sekhem and of the spirits of Annu. I sail among them, and I come; I am crowned, I am become a shining one, I am mighty, I am become holy among the gods. I am the god Khonsu who driveth back all that opposeth him."

The following rubric to this chapter is found in a papyrus at Paris; see Naville, *Todtenbuch*, Bd. II., Bl. 185:—

If this chapter be known, the purified one shall come forth by day after his burial, and he shall change his forms at his heart's desire. He shall dwell among the servants of Un-nefer, and he shall be satisfied with the food of Osiris, and with the meals of the tomb. He shall behold the disk of the Sun, and shall travel over the earth with Ra. He shall be triumphant before Osiris, and there shall no evil thing get dominion over him for ever and for all eternity and for ever.

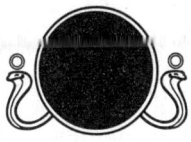

PLATE

28

ignette: A heron.

THE CHAPTER OF CHANGING INTO A HERON.

Saith Osiris, the scribe Ani: "I have gotten dominion over the beasts which are brought for sacrifice, with the knife held at their heads and their hair, for those who dwell in their emerald [fields], the ancient and the shining ones who make ready the hour of Osiris Ani, triumphant in peace. He maketh slaughter upon earth, and I make slaughter upon earth. I am strong, and I have passed along the lofty path [which leadeth] unto heaven. I have made myself pure, with long strides I have gone unto my city, holding on my way to Sepu (?). I have stablished [the one who is] in Unnu. I have set the gods upon their places, and I have made glorious the temples of those who live in their shrines. I know the goddess Nut, I know the god Tatunen, I know Teshert, I have brought with me their horns. I know Heka, I have heard his words, I am the red calf which is limned with the pen. When they hear [my words], the gods say: 'Let us bow down our faces, and let him come unto us; the light shineth beyond you.' My hour is within my body. I have not spoken [evil] in the place of right and truth, and each day I advance in right and truth. I am shrouded in darkness when I sail up to celebrate the festival of the dead one, and to embalm the Aged one, the guardian of the earth—I the Osiris, the scribe Ani, triumphant! I have not entered into the hiding places of the starry deities. I have ascribed glory unto Osiris. I have pacified the heart of the gods who follow after him. I have not felt fear Of those who cause terror, even those who dwell in their own lands. Behold, I am exalted upon [my] resting place upon my throne. I am Nu, and I shall never be overthrown by the Evil-doer. I am the god Shu who sprang from unformed matter. My soul is god; my soul is eternity. I am the creator of darkness, and I appoint unto it a resting place in the uttermost parts of heaven. I am the prince of eternity, I am the exalted one [in] Nebu. I grow young in [my] city, (17) I grow young in my homestead. My name is 'Never-failing.' My name is 'Soul, Creator of Nu, who maketh his abode in the underworld.' My nest is not seen, and I have not broken my egg. I am lord of millions of years- I have made my nest in the uttermost parts of heaven. I have come down unto the earth of Seb. I have done away with my faults. I have seen my father as the lord of Shautat. As concerning Osiris Ani, may his body dwell in Annu; may it be manifested unto those who are with the Shining One in the place of burial in Amenta."

Vignette: A human head springing from a lotus in a pool of water.

THE CHAPTER OF] CHANGING INTO A LOTUS. Saith Osiris Ani: "I am the pure lotus which cometh forth from the god of light, the guardian of the nostrils of Ra, the guardian of the nose

PLATE 28

of Hathor. I advance and I hasten after him who is Horus. I am, the pure one who cometh forth from the field."

Vignette: A god with a disk upon his head.

[Tim, CHAPTER OF] CHANGING INTO THE GOD WHO GIVETH LIGHT IN THE DARKNESS. Saith Osiris, the scribe Ani, triumphant: I am the girdle of the robe of the god Nu, which shineth and sheddeth light, which abideth in his presence and sendeth forth light into the darkness, which knitteth together the two fighters who live in my body through the mighty spell of the words of my mouth, which raiseth up him that hath fallen—for he who was with him in the valley of Abtu hath fallen—and I rest. I have remembered him. I have carried away the god Hu from my city wherein I found him, and I have led away the darkness captive by my might. I have upheld the Eye [of the Sun] when its power waned at the coming of the festival of the, fifteenth day, and I have weighed Sut in the heavenly mansions beside the Aged one who is with him. I have endowed Thoth in the House of the Moon-god with all that is needful for the coming of the festival of the fifteenth day. I have carried off the *ureret* crown; right and truth are in my body. The months are of emerald and crystal. My homestead is among the sapphire furrows. I am the lady who sheddeth light in darkness. I have come to give forth light in darkness, and lo! it is lightened and made bright. I have illumined the blackness and I have overthrown the destroyers. I have made obeisance unto those who are in darkness, and I have raised up those who wept and who had bidden their faces and had sunk down. Then did they look upon me. I am the Lady, and I will not let you hear concerning me."

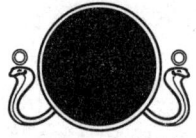

PLATES

29-30

Vignette (PLATE 29.): Ani and his wife standing with hands raised in adoration before the god Thoth, who has *ankh*, "life," upon his knees, and is seated on a pylon-shaped throne.

THE CHAPTER OF NOT DYING A SECOND TIME. Saith Osiris Ani, triumphant: "Hail, Thoth! What is it that hath happened unto the holy children of Nut? They have done battle, they have upheld strife, they have done evil, they have created the fiends, they have made slaughter, they have caused trouble; in truth, in all their doings the mighty have worked against the weak. Grant, O might of Thoth, that that which the god Tmu hath decreed [may be done]! And thou regardest not evil, nor art thou provoked to anger when they bring their years to confusion and throng in and push to disturb their months; for in all that they have done unto thee they have worked iniquity in secret. I am thy writing palette, O Thoth, and I have brought unto thee thine ink jar. I am not of those who work iniquity in their secret places; let not evil happen unto me."

Saith Osiris, the scribe Ani: "Hail, Tmu! What manner [of land] is this into which I have come? It hath not water, it hath not air; it is deep unfathomable, it is black as the blackest night, and men wander helplessly therein. In it a man may not live in quietness of heart; nor may the longings of love be satisfied therein. But let the state of the shining ones be given unto me for water and for air and for the satisfying of the longings of love, and let quietness of heart be given unto me for bread and for ale. The god Tmu hath decreed that I shall see his face, and that I shall not suffer from the things which pain him. May the gods hand on their thrones for millions of years. Thy throne hath descended unto thy son Horus. The god Tmu hath decreed that his course shall be among the holy princes. In truth, he shall rule over thy throne, and he shall be heir of the throne of the dweller in the Lake of Fire. It hath been decreed that in me he shall see his likeness, and that my face shall look upon the lord Tmu. How long then have I to live? It is decreed that thou shalt live for millions of millions of years, a life of millions of years. May it be granted that I pass on unto the holy princes, for I am doing away with all that I did when this earth came into being from Nu , and when it sprang from the watery abyss even as it was in the days of old. I am Fate (?) and Osiris, and I have changed my form into the likeness of divers serpents . Man knoweth not, and the gods cannot see, the two-fold beauty which I have made for Osiris, who is greater than all the gods. I have granted that he [shall rule] in the mount of the dead . Verily his son Horus is seated upon the throne of the dweller in the double Lake of Fire, as his heir. I have set his throne in the boat of millions of years. Horus is established upon his throne, amid the friends [of Osiris] and all that belonged unto him. Verily the soul of Sut, which is greater than all the gods, hath departed to [Amenta]. May it be granted that I bind his soul in the divine boat at my will O my Osiris, thou hast done for me that which thy father Ra did for thee. May I abide upon the earth lastingly; may I keep possession of my throne; may my heir be strong; may my tomb and my friends who are upon earth flourish; may my enemies be given over to destruction and to the shackles of the goddess Serq! I am thy son, and Ra is my father . For me likewise hast thou made life, strength and health. Horus is established upon his throne. Grant that the days of my life may come unto worship and honour."

Appendix: From the fragmentary copy of this chapter which M. Naville has published in his *Todtenbuch*, Bd. L, Bll. 198, 199, it is clear that the text given in the papyrus of Ani forms only about one-half of it, and that its contents refer to the glorious state of the deceased, who lives again in the form of Horus. He enters among the revered dead; shouts of joy ascend in Suten-henen, and gladness reigns in Naarutef he hath inherited the throne of Osiris, and ruleth the whole earth, and the company of the gods are content thereat; the god Sut feareth him; all sorts and conditions of men both dead and living come before him, and bow down in homage when they behold him; the god hath made all to fear him; Sut cometh unto him with head bent low to the earth; the deceased breaketh and turneth up the earth in blood in Suten-henen; (compare Chap. XVIII., §G); his name shall endure for millions of millions of years; his name shall abide in Suten-henen, and he shall wear the mighty *atef* crown upon his head for millions, and hundreds of thousands, and tens of thousands, and thousands, and hundreds, and tens of years; bread, ale, oxen, wild fowl, all good and pure things and fresh water from the river shall in abundance be offered unto him, *etc.* From the concluding lines we find that the chapter was to be recited over a figure of the god

Horus made of lapis-lazuli, which was to be placed near the neck of the deceased, and which was supposed to give him power upon earth with men, gods, and the shining spirits; the effect upon him would, moreover, be exceedingly beneficial if it were recited in the underworld.

Vignette I. (PLATE XXX.): The god Osiris, bearded and wearing the id white crown, stands in a shrine the roof of which is surmounted by a hawk's head and uraei; at the back of his neck hangs the *menat* (see above p. 245), and in his hands he holds the crook, sceptre, and flail, emblems of royalty, power, and dominion. Behind him stands the goddess Isis, who rests her right hand upon his right shoulder; in her left hand she holds the sign of life. Before Osiris, upon a lotus flower, stand the four children of Horus, the gods of the cardinal points, Mestha, Hapi, Tuamautef, and Qebhsennuf.

Vignette II. (PLATE XXIX.): Ani and his wife Thuthu standing, with hands raised in adoration to Osiris, before a table of offerings.

THE CHAPTER OF ENTERING INTO THE HALL OF DOUBLE RIGHT AND TRUTH: A HYMN OF PRAISE TO OSIRIS, THE DWELLER IN AMENTET. Osiris, the scribe Ani, triumphant, saith: "I have come and I have drawn nigh to see thy beauties; my two hands are raised in adoration of thy name Right and Truth. I have drawn nigh unto the place where the acacia tree groweth not, where the tree thick with leaves existeth not, and where the ground yieldeth neither herb nor grass. And I have entered in unto the place of secret and hidden things, 1 have held converse with the god Sut Osiris, the scribe Ani, hath entered into the House of Osiris, and he hath seen the hidden and secret things which are therein. The holy rulers of the pylons are in the form of shining ones. Anubis spake unto him with the speech of man when he came from Ta-mera, saying, 'He knoweth our paths and our cities, I have been pacified, and the smell of him is to me even as the smell of one of you.'"

Ani saith unto him: "I am Osiris, the scribe Ani, triumphant in peace, triumphant! I have drawn nigh to behold the great gods, and I feed upon the meals of sacrifice whereon their *kas* feed. I have been to the boundaries [of the lands] of the Ram, the lord of Tattu, and he hath granted that I may come forth as a bennu bird and that I may have the power of speech. I have passed through the river-flood. I have made offerings with incense. I have made my way by the side of the thick-leaved tree of the children (?). I have been in Abtu in the House of Satet. I have flooded and I have sunk the boat of my enemies. I have sailed forth upon the Lake in the *neshem* boat. I have seen the noble ones of Kam-ur. I have been in Tattu, and I have constrained myself to silence. I have set the divine Form upon his two feet. I have been with the god Pa-tep-tu-f, and I have seen the dweller in the Holy Temple. I have entered into the House Of Osiris, and I have arrayed myself in the apparel of him who is therein. I have entered into Re-stau, and I have beheld the hidden things which are therein. I have been swathed, but I found for myself a thoroughfare. I have entered into An-aarut-f, and I have clothed my body with the apparel which is therein. The *antu* unguent of women hath been given unto me Verily, Sut spake unto me the things which concern himself, and I said, I Let the thought of the trial of the balance by thee be even within our hearts.'"

The majesty of the god Anubis saith: "Dost thou know the name of this door to declare it unto me?" Osiris, the scribe Ani, triumphant, triumphant in peace, saith: "'Driven away of Shu' is the name of this door." Saith the majesty of the god Anubis: "Dost thou know the name of the upper leaf and of the lower leaf

144

thereof?" [Osiris, the scribe Ani, triumphant in peace saith]:'" Lord
of right and truth, [standing] upon his 'two feet' is the name of
the upper leaf, and 'Lord of might and power, dispenser of cattle'
[is the name of the lower leaf]."[The majesty of the god Anubis
saith]: "Pass thou, for thou knowest [the names] , O Osiris, the
scribe, teller of the divine offerings of all the gods of Thebes, Ani,
triumphant, lord to be revered."

The usual introduction to the CXXVth Chapter reads (see
Naville, *Todtenbuch*, Bd. I., Bl. 133) as follows:—

I. THE FOLLOWING SHALL BE SAID BY A MAN WHEN
HE COMETH UNTO THE HALL OF DOUBLE RIGHT AND
TRUTH, WHEREIN HE IS PURGED OF ALL THE SINS WHICH
HE HATH DONE, AND WHEREIN HE SEETH THE FACES OF
ALL THE GODS: Hail to thee, great god, the lord of Right and
Truth! I have come unto thee, O my lord, and I have drawn nigh
that I may look upon thy beauties. I know thee, and I know the
names of the forty-two gods who dwell with thee in this Hall of
Double Right and Truth, and that they may set the sinners in the
gives, who live and who feed upon their blood on the day when
the natures of men are accounted before Un-neferu.

In very truth 'Rekhti-merti-f-ent-Maat' is thy name. Verily I
have come unto thee, and I bring before thee Right and Truth.
For thy sake I have rejected wickedness. I have done no hurt unto
man, nor have I wrought harm unto beasts. I have committed no
crime in the place of Right and Truth. I have had no knowledge
of evil; nor have I acted wickedly. Each day have I laboured more
than was required of me. My name hath not come forth to the
boat of the Prince. I have not despised God. I have not caused
misery; nor have I worked affliction. I have done not that which
God doth abominate. I have caused no wrong to be done to the
servant by his master. I have caused none to feel pain. I have
made [no man] to weep. I have not committed murder; nor have

I ever bidden any man "to slay on my behalf. I have not wronged the people. I have not filched that which hath been offered in the temples; nor have I purloined the cakes of the gods. I have not carried away the offerings made unto the blessed dead. I have not committed fornication, nor have I defiled my body. I have not added unto nor have I minished the offerings which are due. I have not stolen from the orchards; nor have I trampled down the fields. I have not added to the weight of the balance; nor have I made light the weight in the scales. I have not snatched the milk from the mouth of the babe. I have not driven the cattle from their pastures. I have not snared the water-fowl of the gods. I have not caught fishes with bait of their own bodies. I have not turned back water at its springtide. I have not broken the channel of running water. I have not quenched the flame in its fulness. I have not disregarded the seasons for the offerings which are appointed; I have not turned away the cattle set apart for sacrifice. I have not thwarted the processions of the god. 1 am pure. I am pure. I am pure. I am pure. I am pure with the purity of the great Bennu bird which is in Suten-henen; for, lo! I am the nostrils of the lord of the winds who maketh all men to live on the day when the eye of the sun becometh full in Annu, in the second month of the season of coming forth until the end thereof, in the presence of the lord of this earth. I behold the eye of the sun wax full in Annu. May no evil happen unto me in this land in the Hall of Double Right and Truth, because I know, even I, the names of the gods who live therein and who are the followers of the great god."

PLATES

31-32

Vignettes: The Hall of Double Right and Truth, wherein Ani has to address severally the forty-two gods, who are seated in a row in the middle of the, hall. At each end is a door that on the right is called "Neb-Maat-heri-tep-retui-f" and that on the left "Neb-pehti-thesu-menment." On the centre of the roof, which is crowned with a series of uraei and feathers emblematic of Maat, is a seated deity with hands extended, the right over the eye of Horus and the left over a pool (see the Vignette of Plate 8. On the right, at the end of the hall (Plate 32.), are four small vignettes, in which are depicted: Two seated figures of the goddess Maat, with emblematic of Right and Truth, on the head, and sceptres and emblems of life in the right and left hands. Osiris, seated, wearing the *atef* crown, and holding in his hands the crook and flail. Before him, by the side of an altar of offerings, stands Ani, with both hands raised in adoration. A balance with the heart, symbolizing the conscience of Ani, in one scale, and emblematic of Right and Truth, in the other. Beside the balance is the tri-formed monster Amemit. Thoth, ibis-headed, seated on a pylon-shaped pedestal, painting a large feather of Maat.

[THE NEGATIVE CONFESSION.]

1. Ani saith: "Hail, thou whose strides are long, who comest forth from Annu, I have not done iniquity."

2. "Hail, thou who art embraced by flame, who comest forth from Kheraba, I have not robbed with violence."

3. "Hail, Fentiu, who comest forth from Khemennu, I have not stolen."

4. "Hail, Devourer of the Shade, who comest forth from Qernet, I have done no murder; I have done no harm."

5. "Hail, Nehau, who comest forth from Re-stau, I have not defrauded offerings."

6. "Hail, god in the form of two lions, who comest forth from heaven, I have not minished oblations."

7. "Hail, thou whose eyes are of fire, who comest forth from Saut, I have not plundered the god."

8. "Hail, thou Flame, which comest and goest, I have spoken no lies."

9. "Hail, Crusher of bones, who comest forth from Suten-henen, I have not snatched away food."

10. "Hail, thou who shootest forth the Flame, who comest forth from Het-Ptah-ka, I have not caused pain."

11. "Hail, Qerer, who comest forth from Amentet, I have not committed fornication."

12. "Hail, thou whose face is turned back, who comest forth from thy hiding place, I have not caused shedding of tears."

13. "Hail, Bast, who comest forth from the secret place, I have not dealt deceitfully."

14. "Hail, thou whose legs are of fire, who comest forth out of the darkness, I have not transgressed."

15. "Hail, Devourer of Blood, who comest forth from the block of slaughter, I have not acted guilefully."

16. "Hail, Devourer of the inward parts, who comest forth from Mabet, I have not laid waste the ploughed land."

17. "Hail, Lord of Right and Truth, who comest forth from the city of Right and Truth, I have not been an eavesdropper."

18. "Hail, thou who dost stride backwards, who comest forth from the city of Bast, I have not set my lips in motion [against any man]."

19. "Hail, Sertiu, who comest forth from Annu, I have not been angry and wrathful except for a just cause."

20. "Hail, thou. being of two-fold wickedness, who comest forth from Ati (?) I have not defiled the wife of any man."

21. "Hail, thou two-headed serpent, who comest forth from the torture-chamber, I have not defiled the wife of any man."

22. "Hail, thou who dost regard what is brought unto thee, who comest forth from Pa-Amsu, I have not polluted myself."

23. "Hail, thou Chief of the mighty, who comest forth from Amentet, I have not caused terror."

24. "Hail, thou Destroyer, who comest forth from Kesiu, I have not transgressed."

25. "Hail, thou who orderest speech, who comest forth from Urit, I have not burned with rage."

26. "Hail, thou Babe, who comest forth from Uab, I have not stopped my ears against the words of Right and Truth."

27. "Hail, Kenemti, who comest forth from Kenemet, I have not worked grief"

28. "Hail, thou who bringest thy offering, I have not acted with insolence."

29. "Hail, thou who orderest speech, who comest forth from Unaset, I have not stirred up strife."

30. "Hail, Lord of faces, who comest forth from Netchfet, I have not judged hastily."

31. "Hail, Sekheriu, who comest forth from Utten, I have not been an eavesdropper."

32. "Hail, Lord of the two horns, who comest forth from Saïs, I have not multiplied words exceedingly."

33. "Hail, Nefer-Tmu, who comest forth from Het-Ptah-ka, I have done neither harm nor ill."

PLATE 32

34. "Hail, Tmu in thine hour, who comest forth from Tattu, I have never cursed the king."

35. "Hail, thou who workest with thy will, who comest forth from Tebu, I have never fouled the water."

36. "Hail, thou bearer of the sistrum, who comest forth from Nu, I have not spoken scornfully."

37. "Hail, thou who makest mankind to flourish, who comest forth from Saïs, I have never cursed God."

38. "Flail, Neheb-ka, who comest forth from thy hiding place, I have not stolen."

39. "Hail, Neheb-nefert, who comest forth from thy hiding place, I have not defrauded the offerings of the gods."

40. "Hail, thou who dost set in order the head, who comest forth from thy shrine, I have not plundered the offerings to the blessed dead."

41. "Hail, thou who bringest thy arm, who comest forth from the city of Maati, I have not filched the food of the infant, neither have I sinned against the god of my native town."

42. "Hail, thou whose teeth are white, why comest forth from Ta-she, I have not slaughtered with evil intent the cattle of the god."

The following version of the Negative Confession is given in the Nebseni Papyrus (Naville, *Todtenbuch*, Bd. I., Bll. 134, 135), showing important variations in the text and in the order in which the gods are addressed.

Khemennu, I have not made any to suffer pain. Hail, Devourer of Shades, who comest forth from [thy] retreat, I have not robbed. Hail, thou whose limbs are terrible to look upon, who comest forth from Restau, I have done no murder. Hail, thou god who art in the form of two lions, who comest forth from heaven, I have not defrauded offerings. Hail, thou god whose two eyes are of fire, who comest forth from Sekhem, I have not done harm. Hail, Fiery god, who comest and goest, I have not robbed God. Hail, Crusher of Bones, who comest forth from Suten-henen, I have told no lies. Hail, thou who shootest thyself forth from the flame, who comest forth from Het-Ptah-ka, I have not snatched away food. Hail, Qerti, who comest forth from Amentet, I have not worked affliction. Hail, thou whose teeth are white, who comest forth from Ta-she, I have not transgressed. Hail, Devourer of blood, who comest forth from the block, I have not slaughtered the cattle which are set apart for the gods. Hail, Devourer of the inward parts, who comest forth from Mabit, I have done no evil. Hail, lord of Right and Truth, who comest forth from Maati, I have not laid waste the ploughed lands. Hail, Strider, who comest forth from Bast, I have not been an eavesdropper. Hail, Aaati, who comest forth from Annu, I have not set my lips in motion against any man. Hail, thou god of two-fold evil, who comest forth from Ati, I have not been angry without a cause. Hail, thou god who art in the likeness of a serpent, who comest forth from the torture-chamber, I have not committed adultery with the wife of any man. Hail, thou who regardest that which is brought before thee, who comest forth from Pa-Amsu, I have not polluted myself Hail, thou mighty Chief, who comest forth from the city of acacia trees, I have not caused

151

terror. Hail, Khemi, who comest forth from Kesui, I have not done that which is abominable. Hail, thou who orderest speech, who comest forth from Urib, I have never uttered fiery words. Hail, thou Babe, who comest forth from the Heq-at nome, I have not stopped my ears against the words of Right and Truth. Hail, thou who orderest speech, who comest forth from Unes, I have not stirred up strife. Hail, Bast, who comest forth from the secret city, I have not caused [any] to weep. Hail, thou whose face is turned behind thee, I have not lusted, nor have I committed fornication, nor have I done any other abominable thing. Hail, Blazing feet, who comest forth from the darkness, I have not avenged myself Hail, Kenemti, who comest forth from Kenemti, I have never worked grief. Hail, thou who bringest thy offering, who comest forth from Sau, I have not acted insolently. Hail, lord of faces, who comest forth from Tchefet, I have never judged hastily. Hail, Sekheriu, who comest forth from Unth, I have not transgressed, nor have I vexed or angered God. Hail, lord of the two horns, who comest forth from Saui, I have not multiplied my speech overmuch. Hail, Nefer-Tmu, who comest forth from Het-Ptah-ka, I have done no harm nor have I done evil. Hail, Tmu in thine hour, who comest forth from Tattu, I have not worked treason. Hail, thou who workest in thy heart, who comest forth from Tebtu, I have never befouled the water. Hail, thou bearer of the sistrum, who comest forth from Nu, I have not spoken scornfully. Hail, thou who dost make mankind to flourish, who comest forth from thy hall, I have not cursed God. Hail, Neheb-nefert, who comest forth from I have not behaved myself with arrogance. Hail, Neheb-kau, who comest forth from thy city, I have not been overweeningly proud. Hail, Tcheser-tep, who comest forth from thy hiding place, I have never magnified my condition beyond what was fitting. Hail, thou who bringest thine arm, who comest forth from Aukert, I have never slighted the god in my town."

In the Nebseni papyrus (Naville, *Todtenbuch*, Bd. I., Bll. 137, 138), the CXXVth Chapter ends as follows:—

"Homage to you, O ye gods, I know You, and I know your names. Cast me not down to your knives of slaughter, and bring not my wickedness into the presence of the god whom ye follow, and let not the time of my failings come before you. I pray you, declare me right and true in the presence of the universal God, because I have done that which is right and true in Ta-mera; I have not cursed the god . . .

"Homage to you, O ye gods who live in your hall Of Right and Truth, and who have no evil in your bodies, who feed on your own substance in the presence of Horus who liveth in his disk, deliver ye me from Baabi, who feedeth on the inwards of the mighty ones on the day of the great judgment which shall be holden by you. I have come unto you; I have committed no faults; I have not sinned; I have done no evil; I have accused no man falsely; therefore let nothing be done against me. I live in right and truth, and I feed my heart upon right and truth. That which men have bidden I have done, and the gods are satisfied thereat. I have pacified the god, for I have done his will. I have given bread unto the hungry and water unto those who thirst, clothing unto the naked, and a boat unto the shipwrecked mariner. I have made holy offerings unto the gods; and I have given meals of the tomb to the sainted dead. O, then, deliver ye me, and protect me; accuse me not before the great god. I am pure of mouth, and I am pure of hands. May those who see me say, 'Come in peace, come in peace.' For I have heard the speech which the Ass held with the Cat in the House of Hept-re. 1 have borne witness before him [the god] and he hath given judgment. I have beheld the dividing of the persea trees within Re-stau. I offer up prayers in the presence of the gods, knowing that which concerneth them. I have come forward to make a declaration of right and truth, and to place the balance upon its supports within the groves of amaranth. Hail, thou who art exalted upon thy resting place, thou lord of the *atef* crown, who declarest thy name as the lord of the winds, deliver thou me from thine angels of destruction, who make dire deeds to happen and calamities to arise, and who have no covering upon their faces, because I have done right and truth, O thou Lord of right and truth. I am pure, in my fore-parts have I been made clean, and in my hinder parts have I been purified; my reins have been bathed in the Pool of right and truth, and no member of my body was wanting. I have been purified in the pool of the south. I have rested in Hemet, on the north of the field of the grasshoppers, wherein the holy mariners do purify themselves in the night season, that they may pacify (?) the heart of the gods after I have passed over it by night and by day. May the gods say unto me, 'We let him come,' and they say unto me, 'Who art thou, and what is thy name?' My name is 'I grew among the flowers, dwelling in the olive tree.' Then shall they say unto me, 'Pass on straightway.' I have passed by the city on the north of the groves, and the gods say, 'What didst thou see there?' [I saw] the Leg and the Thigh. 'What hadst thou to do with them?' I saw rejoicings in the lands of the Fenkhu. 'What did they give thee?' They gave me a flame of fire together with a crystal tablet. 'What didst thou therewith?' I burned it at the place of Maati together with the things of the night. 'What didst thou find there at the place of Maati?' A sceptre of flint which maketh a man to prevail. 'What then is [the name] of this sceptre of flint?' 'Giver of winds' is its name. 'What then didst thou unto the flame of fire with the tablet of crystal after thou didst bury it?' I uttered words over it, I made adjuration thereby, I quenched the fire, and I used the tablet to create a pool of water. 'Come, then, pass through the door of this Hall of two-fold Maati, for thou knowest us.' 'I will not let thee enter in over me,' saith the bolt of the door, 'unless thou tell my name.' 'Weight of the place of right and truth' is thy name. I will not let thee pass in by me,' saith the right post of the door, 'unless thou tell my name.' 'Weigher of the labours of right and truth' is thy name. 'I will not let thee enter in by me,' saith the left Post of the door, 'unless thou tell my name.' 'judge of wine' (?) is thy name. 'I will not let thee pass,' saith the threshold of the door, unless thou tell my name.' 'Ox of Seb' is thy name. 'I will not open unto thee,' saith the bolt-socket of the door, 'unless thou tell my name.' 'Flesh of his mother' is thy name. I will not open unto thee,' saith the lock of the door, 'unless thou tell my name.' The *utchat* of Sebek, the Lord of Bakhan, liveth' is thy name. 'I will not open unto thee, and I will not let thee pass over me,' saith the dweller at the door, 'unless thou tell my name.' 'Arm of Shu that placeth itself to protect Osiris' is thy name. 'We will not let thee pass by us,' say the posts of the door, 'unless thou tell our names.' 'Serpent children of Rennut' are your names. 'Thou knowest us, pass thou by us.' 'Thou shalt not tread upon me,' saith the floor of the hall, I unless thou tell my name.' 'I am silent, I am pure.' 'I know not [the names of] thy two feet with which thou wouldst walk upon me; tell them unto me.' '. before Amsu' is the name of my right foot, 'Grief of Nephthys' is the name of my left foot. 'Tread thou upon me, for thou knowest me.' 'I will not question thee,' saith the warder of the door of the hall, unless thou tell my name.' 'Discerner of hearts, searcher of reins' is thy name. I will question thee now. Who is the god that liveth in his hour? Say thou.' The teller of the two lands. 'Who then is the teller of the two lands?' It is Thoth. 'Come then,' saith Thoth, 'come hither.' And I come forward to the test. 'What, now, is thy condition?' I am pure from all evil, I am shielded from the baleful acts of those who live in their days, and I am not among them. 'I have tried thee. Who is he that goeth down into the fire, the walls whereof are [crowned] with uraei, and whose paths are in the lake [of fire]?' He who passeth through it is Osiris. 'Advance thou, in very truth thou hast been tested. Thy bread is in the *utchat*, thine ale is in the *utchat*, and meals of the tomb are brought forth unto thee upon earth from the *utchat*. This hath been decreed for thee.'"

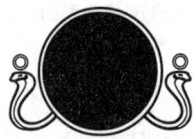

PLATE

32 (continued)

Vignette: The god Nu.
  Text: The hair of Osiris Ani, triumphant, is the hair of Nu.

Vignette: Ra, hawk-headed, and wearing a disk.

Text: The face of Osiris, the scribe Ani, is the face of Ra.

Vignette: The goddess Hathor, wearing disk and horns.

Text: The eyes of Osiris Ani, triumphant, are the eyes of Hathor.

Vignette: The god Ap-uat and standard.

Text: The ears of Osiris Ani, triumphant, are the ears of Ap-uat.

Vignette: The god Anpu, jackal-headed.

Text: The lips of Osiris Ani, triumphant, are the lips of Anpu.

Vignette: The scorpion Serqet, holding the *shen*, and *ankh*.

Text: The teeth of Osiris Ani, triumphant, are the teeth of Serqet.

Vignette: The goddess Isis.

PLATE 32 (continued)

Text: The neck of Osiris Ani, triumphant, is the neck of Isis.

Vignette: The ram-headed god, with uraeus between the horns.

Text: The hands of Osiris Ani, triumphant, are the hands of the Ram, the lord of Tattu.

Vignette: The god Uatchit, serpent-headed.

Text: The shoulder of Osiris Ani, triumphant, is the shoulder of Uatchit.

Vignette: The goddess Mert, with outstretched hands, standing upon the emblem of gold, and having on her head a cluster of plants.

Text: The throat of Osiris Ani, triumphant, is the. blood of Mert.

Vignette: The goddess Neith.

Text: The fore-arms of Osiris Ani, triumphant, are the fore-arms of the lady of Sais.

Vignette: The god Sut.

Text: The backbone of Osiris Ani, triumphant, is the backbone of Sut

Vignette: A god.

Text: The chest of Osiris Ani, triumphant, is the chest of the lords of Kher-aba.

Vignette: A god.

Text: The flesh of Osiris Ani, triumphant, is the flesh of the Mighty One of terror.

Vignette: The goddess Sekhet, lion-headed, wearing a disk.

Text: The reins and back of Osiris Ani, triumphant, are the reins and back of Sekhet.

Vignette: An *utchat* upon a pylon.

Text: The buttocks of Osiris Ani, triumphant, are the buttocks of the Eye of Horus.

Vignette: Osiris, wearing the atef crown and holding the flail and crook.

Text: The privy member of Osiris Ani, triumphant, is the privy member of Osiris.

Vignette: The goddess Nut.

Text: The legs of Osiris Ani, triumphant, are the legs of Nut.

Vignette: The god Ptah.

Text: The feet of Osiris Ani, triumphant, are the feet of Ptah.

Vignette: The star Orion.

Text: The fingers of Osiris Ani, triumphant, are the fingers of Saah (Orion).

Vignette: Three Uraei.

Text: The leg-bones of Osiris Ani, triumphant, are the leg-bones of the living uraei.

The complete version of the XLIInd Chapter of the Book of the Dead, referring to the identification of the body of Osiris with those of the gods, reads as follows:—

THE CHAPTER OF DRIVING BACK SLAUGHTER IN SUTENHENEN. Saith Osiris: "O land of the sceptre! O white crown of the divine Form! O holy resting place! I am the Child. I am the Child. I am the Child. I am the Child. Hail, thou goddess Aburt! Thou sayest daily, 'The slaughter block is made ready as thou knowest, and thou who wert mighty hast been brought to decay.' I establish those who praise me. I am the holy knot within the tamarisk tree, more beautiful in brightness than yesterday." To be said four times. I am Ra who establish those who praise him. I am the knot within the tamarisk tree, more beautiful in brightness than the disk of yesterday. going forth on this. day. My hair is the hair of Nu. My face is the face of Ra. Mine eyes are the eyes of Hathor. Mine ears are the ears of Ap-uat. My nose is the nose of Khent-sheps. My lips are the lips of Anpu. My teeth are the teeth of Khepera. My neck is the neck of Isis, the divine lady. My hands are the hands of Khnemu, the lord of Tattu. My fore-arms are the fore-arms of Neith, the lady of Saïs. My backbone

158

PLATE 32 (continued)

is the backbone of Sut. My privy member is the privy member of Osiris. My reins are the reins of the lords of Kher-aba. My breast is the breast of the awful and terrible One. My belly and my backbone are the belly and backbone of Sekhet. My buttocks are the buttocks of the eye of Horus. My hips and thighs are the hips and thighs of Nut. My feet are the feet of Ptah. My fingers and leg-bones arc the fingers and leg-bones of the living uraei. There is no member of my body which is not the member of some god. Thoth shieldeth my body altogether, and I am [like] unto Ra every day. None shall seize me by mine arms; none shall drag me away by my hand. And there shall do me hurt neither men, nor gods, nor sainted dead, nor they who have perished, nor any one of those of olden times, nor any mortal, nor human being. I come forth and advance, and my name is unknown. I am yesterday, and my name is 'Seer of millions of years.' I travel, I travel along the path of Horus the judge. I am the lord of eternity; I feel and I have power to perceive. I am the lord of the red crown. I am the Sun's eye, yea, I am in my egg, in my egg. It is granted unto me to live therewith. I am in the Sun's eye, when it closeth, and I live by the strength thereof I come forth and I shine; I enter in and I come to life. I am in the Sun's eye, my seat is on my throne, and I sit thereon within the eye. I am Horus who pass through millions of years. I have governed my throne and I rule it by the words of my mouth; and whether [I] speak or whether [I] keep silence, I keep the balance even. Verily my forms are changed. I am the god Unen, from season unto season; what is mine is within me. I am the only One born of an only One, who goeth round about in his course; 1 am within the eye of the Sun. Things are not evil nor hostile unto me, nor are they against me. I open the door of heaven. I govern my throne, and I give [new] birth to myself on this day. [I am] not the Child who trod the path of yesterday, but I am 'To-day' for untold nations. It is I who make you strong for millions of years, whether ye be in the heaven, or in the earth, or in the south, or in the north, or in the west or in the east; fear of me is in your hearts. I am the pure one who dwell within the sacred eye. I shall not die again. My hour resteth with you, but my forms are within my dwelling-place. I am he who is unknown, and the gods with rose-bright countenances are with me. I am the unveiled one. The season wherein [the god] created heaven for me and enlarged the bounds of the earth and made great the progeny thereof cannot be found Out. My name setteth itself apart and removeth from all evil things through the words which I speak unto you. I am he who riseth and shineth; the wall of walls; the only One, [son] of an only One. Ra never lacketh his form, he never passeth away, he never passeth away. Verily, I say: I am the plant which cometh forth from Nu, and my mother is Nut. Hail, O my Creator, I am he who hath no power to walk, the great knot within yesterday. My power is in my hand. I am not known, [but] I am he who knoweth thee. I cannot be held with the hand, but I am he who can hold thee in his hand. [Hail] O Egg! [Hail] O Egg! I am Horus who live for millions of years, whose flame lighteth upon your faces and blazeth in your hearts. I have the command of my throne, and I advance in mine hour. I have opened the paths, I have turned myself away from all evil. I am (28) the ape of gold, three palms and two fingers [high], which is without legs and without arms, and which dwelleth in the House of Ptah. I go forth even as goeth forth the ape Of gold three palms and two fingers [high], which hath neither legs nor arms, and which dwelleth in the house of Ptah." When [thou] hast said this chapter thou shalt open a way and enter thereon.

PLATE 32 (continued)

PLATE 33

A lake of fire, at each corner of which is seated a dog-headed ape.

Rubric: Osiris Ani, triumphant, is girt about with [fine] raiment, he is shod with white sandals, and he is anointed with very precious *anta* ointment; and a bull, and herbs, and incense, and ducks, and flowers, and ale, and cakes have been offered unto him. And behold, thou shalt limn upon a clean tile the image of a table of offerings in clean colours, and thou shalt bury it in a field whereon swine have not trampled. If this word then be written upon it, he himself shall rise again, and his children's children shall flourish even as Ra flourisheth without ceasing. He shall dwell in favour in the presence of the king among the chiefs, and cakes and cups of drink and portions of meat shall be given unto him upon the table of the great god. He shall not be thrust from any door in Amentet; he shall travel on together with the kings of the north and of the south, and he shall abide with the followers of Osiris near unto Un-nefer, for ever, and for ever, and for ever.

Vignette: A Tet.

THE CHAPTER OF A TET OF GOLD: Osiris Ani, triumphant, saith: "Thou risest, O still heart! Thou shinest, O still heart! Place thou thyself upon my side. I have come arid I have brought unto thee a tet of gold; rejoice thou in it."

Appendix: In the late recension of this chapter (Lepsius, *Todtenbuch*, Bl. 75) the rubric is divided into two parts, which read: "To be recited over a Tet of gold inlaid in sycamore wood, and placed on the neck of the shining one; and he shall pass in through the doors of the underworld by the might of the words here spoken. It shall set him in his place on the day of the new year among the followers of Osiris.

"If this chapter be known by the deceased he shall become perfect in the underworld. He shall not be thrust back at the doors of Amentet; cakes and ale and meat offerings shall be offered unto him upon the altars of Ra, or (as some say) of Osiris Unnefer; and he shall triumph over his foes in the underworld for ever and for ever."

Vignette: A buckle, or tie.

THE CHAPTER OF A BUCKLE OF CARNELIAN. Saith Osiris Ani, triumphant: "The blood of Isis, the charms of Isis, the power of Isis, are a protection unto me, the chief, and they crush that which I abhor."

Appendix: *Rubric:* This chapter shall be said over a buckle of red jasper (*or* carnelian) which hath been dipped in water of *ankham* flowers and inlaid in sycamore wood, and hath been placed on the neck of the shining one. If this chapter be inscribed upon it, it shall become the power of Isis, and it shall protect him; and Horus, the son of Isis, shall rejoice when he seeth it. No way shall be impassable to him, and one hand shall extend unto heaven, and the other unto earth. If this chapter be known [by the deceased] he shall be among those who follow Osiris Unnefer, triumphant. The gates of the underworld shall be opened unto him, and a homestead shall be given unto him, together with wheat and barley, in the Sekhet-Aaru; and the followers of Horus who reap therein shall proclaim his name as one of the gods who are therein.

Vignette: A heart.

THE CHAPTER OF A HEART OF CARNELIAN. Saith Osiris

PLATE 32 (continued)

Ani, triumphant: "I am the *Bennu*, the soul of Ra, and the guide of the gods into the underworld. The souls come forth upon earth to do the will of their *ka's*, and the soul of Osiris Ani cometh forth to do the will of his *ka*."

Vignette: A head-rest.

THE CHAPTER OF THE PILLOW WHICH IS PLACED UNDER THE HEAD OF OSIRIS ANI, TRIUMPHANT, TO WARD OFF WOES FROM THE DEAD BODY OF OSIRIS. [Ani saith]: "Lift up thy head to the heavens, for I have knit thee together triumphantly. Ptah hath overthrown his foes and thine; all his enemies have fallen, and they shall never more rise up again, O Osiris."

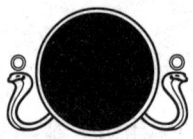

PLATES

33–34

Vignette: The mummy-chamber, arranged as a plan, representing the floor and walls laid flat, in fifteen compartments. In the centre, under a canopy, is place d the bier bearing the mummy of Ani, beside which stands the god Anubis, with hands outstretched over the body. At the foot of the bier kneels the goddess Isis, and at the head the goddess Nephthys, each being accompanied by a flame of fire, which is placed in the compartment immediately behind her. The Tet occupies the compartment immediately above the bier, and the jackal—emblematic of Anubis or Ap-uat—couchant on the tomb, with a sceptre having pendent *menats*—occupies the compartment below. The four children of Horus, or gods of the cardinal points—Mestha, Hapi, Tuamautef, and Qebhsennuf— stand in the corners of the four adjoining compartments. In each of the two upper and outer compartments is the human-headed bird emblematic of the soul, standing on a pylon, the one on the right being turned to the west or setting sun, the other on the left facing the east or rising sun. In the right lower compartment stands the figure of the Perfected Soul; in the corresponding compartment on the left is a Ushabti figure.

[Isis saith:] "I have come to be a protector unto thee. I waft unto thee air for thy nostrils, and the north wind, which cometh forth from the god Tmu, unto thy nose have made whole thy lungs. I have made thee to be like unto a god. Thine enemies have fallen beneath thy feet. (5 6) Thou hast been made victorious in Nut, and thou art mighty to prevail with the gods."

[Nephthys saith:] "I have gone round about to protect thee, brother Osiris; 1 have come to be a protector unto thee. [My strength shall be behind thee, my strength shall be behind thee, for ever. Ra hath heard thy cry, and the gods have granted that thou shouldst be victorious. Thou art raised up, and thou art victorious over that which hath been done unto thee. Ptah hath thrown down thy foes, and thou art Horus, the son of Hathor.]"

[The flame of Isis saith:] "I protect thee with this flame, and I drive away him (the foe) from the valley of the tomb, and I drive away the sand from thy feet. I embrace Osiris Ani, who is triumphant in peace and in right and truth."

[The flame of Nephthys saith:] "I have come to hew in pieces. I am not hewn in pieces, nor will I suffer thee to be hewn in pieces. I have come to do violence, but I will not let violence be done unto thee, for I am protecting thee."

[The Tet saith:] "I have come quickly, and I have driven back the footsteps of the god whose face is hidden. I have illumined his sanctuary. I stand behind the sacred Tet or, the day of repulsing disaster. I protect thee, O Osiris."

[Mestha saith:] I am Mestha, thy son, O Osiris Ani, triumphant. I have come to protect thee, and I will make thine abode to flourish everlastingly. I have commanded Ptah, even as Ra himself commanded him."

[Hapi saith:] "I am Hapi thy son, O Osiris Ani, triumphant. I have come to protect thee. Thy head and thy limbs are knit together; and I have smitten down thine enemies beneath thee. I have given unto thee thy head for ever and for ever, O Osiris Ani, triumphant in peace."

[Tuamautef saith:] "I am thy beloved son Horus. I have come to avenge thee, O my father Osiris, upon him that did evil unto thee; and I have put him under thy feet for ever, and for ever, and for ever; O Osiris Ani, triumphant in peace."

[Qebhsennuf saith:] "I am thy son, O Osiris Ani, triumphant. I have come to protect thee. I have collected thy bones, and I have gathered together thy members. [I have brought thy heart and I have placed it upon its throne within thy body. I have made thy house to flourish after thee, O thou who livest for ever.]"

[The bird which faceth the setting sun saith]: "Praise be to Ra when he setteth in the western part of heaven. Osiris Ani, triumphant in peace in the underworld, saith: 'I am a perfected soul,'"

[The bird which faceth the rising sun saith]: "Praise be to Ra when he riseth in the eastern part of heaven from Osiris Ani, triumphant."

[The Perfected Soul saith]: "I am a perfected soul in the holy egg of the *abtu* fish. I am the great cat which dwelleth in the seat of right and truth wherein riseth the god Shu."

[The text near the Ushabti Figure (Chapter VI.) reads]: Osiris Ani, the overseer, triumphant, saith: "Hail, *shabti* figure! If it be decreed that Osiris [Ani] shall do any of the work which is to be done in the underworld, let all that standeth in the way be removed from before him; whether it be to plough the fields, or to fill the channels with water, or to carry sand from [the East to the West]." The *shabti* figure replies: "I will do [it]; verily I am here [when] thou callest."

Vignette: Ani, with both hands raised in adoration, standing before a table of offerings; behind him is his wife holding lotus and other flowers in her left hand.

HERE BEGIN THE CHAPTERS OF THE SEKHET-HETEPU, AND THE CHAPTERS OF COMING FORTH BY DAY, AND OF GOING INTO AND OF COMING OUT FROM THE UNDERWORLD, AND OF ARRIVING IN THE SEKHET AANRU, AND OF BEING IN PEACE IN THE GREAT CITY WHEREIN ARE FRESH BREEZES. Let me have power there. Let me become strong to plough there. Let me reap there. Let me eat there. Let me drink there. [Let me woo there.] And let me do all these things there, even as they are done upon earth.

Saith Osiris Ani, triumphant: "Set hath carried away Horus to see what is being built in the Field of Peace, and he spreadeth the air over the divine soul within the egg in its day. He hath delivered the innermost part of the body of Horus from the holy ones of Akert. Behold I have sailed in the mighty boat on the Lake of Peace. I, even I, have crowned him in the House of Shu. His starry abode reneweth its youth, reneweth its youth. I have sailed on its Lake that I may come unto its cities, and I have drawn nigh It unto the city Hetep. For behold, I repose at the seasons [of Horus]. I have passed through the region of the company of the gods who are aged and venerable. 1 have pacified the two holy Fighters who keep ward upon life. I have done that which is right and fair, and I have brought an offering and have pacified the two holy Fighters. I have cut off the hairy scalp of their adversaries, and I have made aft end of the woes which befel [their] children; I have done away all the evil which came against their souls; I have gotten dominion over it, 1 have knowledge thereof. I have sailed forth on the waters [of the lake] that I may come unto the cities thereof. I have power over my mouth, being furnished [with] charms; let not. [the fiends] get the mastery over me, let them not have dominion over me.

May I be equipped in thy Fields of Peace. What thou wishest that shalt thou do, [saith the god]."

Vignette: The Sekhet-hetepet or "Fields of Peace," surrounded and intersected with streams. They contain the following:

(*a*) Thoth, the scribe of the gods, holding pen and palette, introduces Ani, who is making an offering, and his *ka* to three gods who have the heads of a hare, serpent, and bull respectively, and are entitled *pauti*, "the company of the gods." Ani and a table of offerings in a boat. Ani addressing a hawk standing on a pylon-shaped pedestal, before which are an altar and a god. Three ovals. The legend reads *un em hetep sexet nifu er fent*, "Being at peace in the Field [of Peace], and having air for the nostrils."

(*b*) Ani reaping wheat, with the words *asex Ausar*, "Osiris reaps"; guiding the oxen treading out the corn; standing with hands and holding the *kherp* sceptre, and kneeling before two vessels of red barley and wheat. The hieroglyphics seem to mean, "the food of the shining ones." Three ovals.

(*c*) Ani ploughing with oxen in a part of the Fields of Peace called "Sekhet-aanre"; with the word *sekau*, to plough. The two lines of hieroglyphics read:—

re en hete'et atru 1000 em au-f an t'et usex-f an un remu neb am-f an hefau nebt am-f.

Chapter of the River-horse. The river is one thousand [cubits] in its length. Not can be told its width. Not exist fishes any in it, not [exist] serpents any in it.

(*d*) A boat bearing a flight of steps and floating on a stream; above is the legend *tehefau*, A boat of eight oars, each end shaped like a serpent's head, bearing a flight of steps; at the stern is written and at the bows *meter am Un-nefer*, "the god therein is Un-nefer." The stream which flows on the convex side of the small

172

island is called *ashet pet*, "flood of [heaven]." On the other island is placed a flight of steps, by the side of which is written The space to the left represents the abode of the blessed dead, and is described as:—

duset xu au-sen meh sexef at meh xemt an saku aqeru asexet-sen

The seat of the shining ones. Their length is cubits seven the wheat cubits three the blessed dead who are perfected they reap [it].

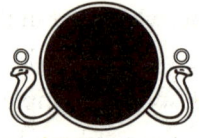

PLATE

37

Vignette: A shrine wherein stands *Sekeri-Ausar neb setait neter aa neb Neter-xert* Seker-Osiris, lord of the hidden place, the great god, the lord of the underworld.

He wears the white crown with feathers, and holds in his hands the sceptre, flail, and crook.

The goddess Hathor, in the form of a hippopotamus, wearing upon her head a disk and horns; in her right hand she holds an unidentified object, and in her left the emblem of life. Before her are tables of meat and drink offerings and flowers. Behind the hippopotamus, the divine cow, Meh-urit, symbolizing the same goddess, looks out from the funeral mountain, wearing the *menat* on her neck. At the foot of the mountain is the tomb; and in the foreground grows a group of flowering plants.

Hathor, lady of Amentet, dweller in the land of Urt, lady of Ta-sert, the Eye of Ra, the dweller in his brow, the beautiful Face in the Boat of Millions of Years . . .